CHARACTER TEXT
FOR P.C.T'UNG & D.E.POLLARD
COLLOQUIAL CHINESE

SIMPLIFIED CHARACTER VERSION

汉语口语

汉字本

PREPARED BY
PING-CHENG T'UNG

ISBN   0 9508572 1 1

Prepared and published by

P.C. T'ung
Department of the Far East
School of Oriental and African Studies
University of London

First published 1983
Reprinted 1986, 1989, 1994

Printed in Hong Kong

CONTENTS

BASIC STROKES OF CHINESE CHARACTERS

Basic Strokes	Examples	Some Variants and Combined Strokes		Examples	
丶	文	丶	✓	小	东
		丶	丶	不	头
一	大	フ	フ	口	五
		ㄱ	ㄱ	习	门
		フ	フ	刀	力
		フ	フ	又	条
		一	一	买	你
		し	し	没	朵
		し	し	请	说
		ろ	ろ	及	建
		了	了	乃	阿
		乙	乙	亿	吃
		て	て	飞	气
丨	中	亅	亅	小	才
		し	し	比	衣
		ㄴ	ㄴ	山	忙
		し	し	儿	也
		ㄅ	ㄅ	马	弓
丿	人	丿	丿	儿	月
		丶	丶	后	他
		ㄥ	ㄥ	么	去
		く	く	女	巡
丶	入	乁	乁	这	走
丶	汉				
丿	家	乀	乀	我	代
		乚	乚	心	必

GENERAL RULES OF STROKE-ORDER OF CHINESE CHARACTERS

1. From top to bottom

   Examples: | 三 | 一 二 三 | 高 | 亠 古 高 |

2. From left to right

   Examples: | 你 | 亻 你 | 啊 | 口 吖 啊 |

3. From outside to inside

   Examples: | 同 | 门 同 | 风 | 几 风 |

4. Left-falling precedes right-falling

   Examples: | 人 | 丿 人 | 又 | 乛 又 |

5. Horizontal precedes crossing vertical or other downstroke

   Examples: | 十 | 一 十 | 天 | 二 天 天 |

6. Box precedes crossing vertical or other downstroke

   Examples: | 中 | 口 中 | 史 | 口 史 史 |

7. Bottom horizontal last

   Examples: | 王 | 二 王 王 | 正 | 丁 下 正 正 |

8. Inside precedes the sealing stroke

   Examples: | 日 | 冂 日 日 | 国 | 冂 国 国 国 |

9. Middle precedes the two sides

   Examples: | 小 | 亅 小 小 | 水 | 亅 水 水 |

10. Top left dot first; top right dot last

    Examples: | 为 | 丶 丿 为 为 | 找 | 扌 找 找 |

天	tiān (N) sky; heaven; weather; day (M) for days	也	yě (A) also, too; either
气	qì　　　[氣] (N) air; breath	们	mén　　*　[們] plural suffix for personal pronouns and nouns denoting persons
很	hěn (A) very; quite	忙	máng (SV) busy
好	hǎo (SV) good; well; fine (IE) all right, O.K.	昨	zuó　　* yesterday 昨天
冷	lěng (SV) cold	呢	ne (P) particle for follow-up questions
吗	ma　　[嗎] (P) question particle	早	zǎo (SV) early (IE) good morning!
不	bù (A) not; no, not so	啊	a (P) question and modal particle
热	rè　　[熱] (SV) hot (of weather); warm	都	dōu　　[都] (A) all; both; in all cases
今	jīn　　* at present, now 今天 today	请	qǐng　　[請] (V) to request; to invite (IE) (will you) please
真	zhēn (A) truly, really (AT) real, true	坐	zuò (V) to sit; to travel by
我	wǒ (PN) I, me	再	zài (A) again, once more
你	nǐ (PN) you	见	jiàn　　[見] (V) to see; to meet

您	nín (PN) you (polite form)	她	tā (PN) she, her
他	tā (PN) he, him		

* bound elements —— only occur as constituents of words; do not occur
　　　　　　　　independently

[　] Full-form

STROKE-ORDER

天　一　二　于　天
气　丿　𠂉　气　气
很　彳　丿　彡　彳
　　艮　フ　ヨ　ヨ　艮　艮　艮
好　女　く　女　女
　　子　フ　了　子
冷　冫　丶　冫
　　令　丿　人　仌　今　令
吗　口　丶　口　口
　　马　フ　马　马
不　一　丆　オ　不
热　扌　一　十　扌
　　丸　丿　九　丸
　　灬　丶　灬　灬
今　丿　人　亼　今
真　一　十　广　方　𥄚　直　直　真　真
我　丿　二　于　扌　抈　我　我
你　亻　丿　亻
　　尔　丿　𠂊　𠂆　尔　尔
也　フ　九　也

们　亻　丿　亻
　　门　丶　冫　门
忙　忄　丨　忄　忄
　　亡　丶　亠　亡
昨　日　丨　冂　月　日
　　乍　丿　𠂉　仠　乍　乍
呢　口　丶　冂　口
　　尼　フ　コ　尸　尸　尼
早　丶　冂　日　旦　早
啊　口　丶　冂　口
　　阝　ㄋ　阝
　　可　一　口　可
都　者　一　十　土　耂　者　者　者
　　阝　ㄋ　阝
请　讠　丶　讠
　　青　一　二　𡗗　𡗗　青　青　青
坐　丶　人　𠘧　𠓦　竺　坐
再　一　厂　冂　冄　再　再
　　　　丿　冄　冄　再
见　丨　冂　贝　见

2

您　你　′　亻　亻′　亻′′　你　你　你　　　他　′　亻　亻′　仲　他
心　′　心　心　心　　　　　　　　　　　她　く　女　女　如　如　她

VOCABULARY

Noun (N)

天气　tiānqi　weather

Time words (TW)

今天　jīntiān　today

昨天　zuótiān　yesterday

Pronouns (PN)

我　wǒ　I, me

你　nǐ　you

您　nín　you (polite form)

他　tā　he, him

她　tā　she, her

我们　wǒmen　we, us

你们　nǐmen　you (plural)

他们
她们　tāmen　they, them

Stative verbs (SV)

好　hǎo　good; fine, all right

冷　lěng　cold

热　rè　hot

忙　máng　busy

早　zǎo　early

Adverbs (A)

很　hěn　very, quite

不　bù　not

真　zhēn　truly, really

也　yě　also, too, either, as well

都　dōu　all, both

Particles (P)

吗　ma　question particle

呢　ne　particle for follow-up question

啊　a　question and modal particle

Idiomatic expressions (IE)

早！　zǎo　good morning!

请坐　qǐng zuò　please sit down

请　qǐng　(will you) please

你好！　nǐ hǎo　How do you do? How are you?

再见　zàijiàn　goodbye

3

(1) 天气很好!
     冷吗? 不冷。
     热吗? 不热。

(2) 今天真冷!
     我很冷,你冷不冷?
     我也很冷。

(3) 你们不忙吗?
     今天不忙,昨天很忙,你们呢?
     我们今天也不忙。

DIALOGUES

(1) A: 早啊!
     B: 早!天气真好。
     A: 真好,不冷不热。
     B: 你们都好吗?
     A: 都好,请坐,请坐。
     B: 好、好。

(2) A: 好啊!
     B: 你好!
     A: 天气真冷!
     B: 真冷,你们忙不忙?
     A: 我们都很忙,你们呢?
     B: 我们也都很忙,再见!
     A: 再见,再见!

(3) A: 昨天真热!
     B: 热?!
     A: 您不热啊?
     B: 我不热。
     A: 真不热吗?
     B: 真不热!

4

SPEECH PATTERNS

(1) Contrastive sentences with stative verbs

Pattern: Topic/subject (neg) SV

昨天　　　　　　冷，
今天　　　　　　热。

1. 冷不好，热好。　　　　　　3. 你忙，我忙，他不忙。

2. 他冷，我不冷。

(2) Stative verbs with adverbial modifiers

Pattern: Topic/subject (A) (A) (A) SV

天气　　　　　　　　真　好。
他们　　都　不　很　忙。

1. 今天很冷。　　　　　　4. 天气很不好。

2. 他们都很冷。　　　　　　5. 他们不都很忙。

3. 我们也都很冷。

Contrast:
$\left\{\begin{array}{l}\text{不很}\\\text{很不}\end{array}\right.$ 天气不很好。
天气很不好。
$\left\{\begin{array}{l}\text{不都}\\\text{都不}\end{array}\right.$ 他们不都忙。
他们都不忙。

(3) Three types of questions

(a) Questions with the interrogative particle ma

Pattern:　　　Statement　+　P?
天气 好　　吗？

1. A: 今天冷吗？　　　　B: 很冷。

2. A: 他们都好吗？　　　B: 都好。

3. A：你不热吗？   B：我不热。

4. A：他们不忙吗？   B：忙！他们都很忙。

(b) Choice-type questions

Pattern:　Topic/subject　　SV　neg SV?
　　　　　　天气　　　　好　不　好？

1. A：今天冷不冷？   B：不很冷。

2. A：你们忙不忙？   B：我们都很忙。

3. A：他热不热？   B：他不热。

(c) Follow-up questions

Pattern:　Topic/subject₁ + comment, topic/subject₂ + ne?
　　　　　　他们　　　都好，　　你们　　　呢？

1. A：你很热吗？   B：不热，你呢？

2. A：你们不忙吗？   B：不忙，你们呢？

3. A：你冷不冷？   B：很冷，你呢？

这	zhè, zhèi　　[這] (SP) this	京	jīng　　　* capital 北京 Peking
是	shì (CLV) to be; to be so (IE) That is so; yes; right	爱	ài　　　　[愛] (V) to like; to love (MV) like to; love to
张	zhāng　　[張] * to extend (M) for paper, table, etc. a common surname	姓	xìng (N) surname (CLV) to be surnamed
华	huá　　*　[華] flowery short for China 中华 Huà a surname	王	wáng (N) king a common surname
同	tóng (SV) same; alike	名	míng　　* name, given name; fame
志	zhì　　　* ambition; will 同志 comrade	字	zì (N) written character; 　　monosyllabic word
中	zhōng　　* middle; centre; amidst short for China 中国	英	yīng　　* flower; brave short for England (U.K.)英国
国	guó　　　[國] (N) country; nation; state * of the state; national	小	xiǎo (SV) small; little; young (　　of age); low (of voice)
人	rén (N) human being, man, person, people	上	shàng (V) to ascend, mount; to go 　　to (L) up; top; upper; above
叫	jiào　　　[叫] (V) to call; to shout; to 　　cause to (CLV) to be called	海	hǎi (N) sea 上海 Shanghai
老	lǎo (SV) old; elderly (A) always; keep .... -ing	姐	jiě　　　* elder sister 姐姐
北	běi (L) north, northern	那	nà, nèi (SP) that in that case

先	xiān (A) first; previously	什	shén * [甚] what
生	shēng (V) to give birth to, be born (SV) raw, unripe; unfamiliar	么	me, mo * [麼] suffix (in 什么 'what'; 这么 'so, in this manner', etc.)
太	tài (A) too, excessively 太太 Mrs; wife	地	dì (N) earth; ground; land; fields
侨	qiáo * [僑] to reside abroad 华侨 overseas Chinese	方	fāng (SV) square * direction; region a surname
美	měi (SV) beautiful, pretty short for America 美国	问	wèn [問] (V) to ask; to enquire (a question)
谁	shéi, shuí [誰] (QW) who, whom	贵	guì [貴] * your (honorific) (SV) expensive, dear
噢	ō [噢] (I) Oh!	夫	fū * man; husband
进	jìn * [進] to enter; to advance	哪	nǎ, něi * (SP) which
吧	ba (P) particle of suggestion		

这	文	、 一 方 文
	辶	、 讠 辶
是	日	丨 冂 冃 日
	疋	一 丁 下 正 疋
张	弓	一 彐 弓
	长	丿 二 长 长
华		丿 亻 亻 化 쑈 华
同		丨 冂 冂 同
志	士	一 十 士
	心	、 心 心 心
中		、 口 口 中
国		丨 冂 冂 冃 闰 国 国 国
人		丿 人
叫		口 叨 叫
老		一 十 土 耂 芳 老
北		丨 十 土 北 北
京		、 亠 古 亠 京 京
爱	爫	丿 丆 爫 爫
	友	一 ナ 方 友
姓		人 女 女 女 好 姓 姓
王		一 二 千 王
名		丿 ク 夕 名
字	宀	丶 冖 宀
	子	乛 了 子
英	艹	一 十 艹
	央	、 口 口 央 央

小		丿 小 小
上		丨 卜 上
海	氵	丶 冫 氵
	每	丿 厂 亡 冇 每 每 每
姐		人 女 女 奵 妍 姐 姐 姐
那		刁 刁 弖 月 那 那
先		丿 一 牛 生 先 先
生		丿 一 牛 生 生
太		一 ナ 大 太
侨		亻 亻 仁 侨 侨 侨
美		、 丷 丷 兰 羊 美 美
谁	讠	丶 讠
	佳	丿 亻 个 广 广 佳 佳
噢	口	
	闱	丿 亻 门 门 闱 闱 闱 闱 闱
	大	一 ナ 大
进		一 二 丰 井 讲 讲 进
吧		口 叨 吧 吧 吧
什		亻 亻 什
么		丿 么 么
地		一 十 土 坩 地 地
方		、 亠 ナ 方
问		、 讠 门 问
贵		丶 口 口 中 虫 串 贵 贵
夫		一 二 丰 夫
哪		口 叨 叨 吗 吗 哪 哪

9

VOCABULARY

Specifiers (SP)

这 zhè, zhèi   this

那 nà, nèi   that

Nouns

同志 tóngzhì   comrade

人 rén   person

爱人 àiren   spouse

姓 xìng   surname

名字 míngzi   given name; full name

小姐 xiáojie   young lady; Miss

先生 xiānsheng   gentleman; Mr; husband

太太 tàitai   lady; Mrs; wife

华侨 huáqiáo   overseas Chinese

地方 dìfang   place

夫人 fūren   madam; Mrs

Classificatory verbs (CLV)

是 shì   to be; to be so

叫 jiào   call; be called

姓 xìng   be surnamed

Stative verbs

老 lǎo   old

小 xiǎo   young; small

Place words (PW)

中国 Zhōngguó   China

北京 Běijīng   Peking

上海 Shànghǎi   Shanghai

英国 Yīngguó   England, GB, UK

美国 Měiguó   America (USA)

Question words (QW)

谁 shéi, shuí   who(m)

什么 shénme   what

哪 nǎ, něi   which

Particle

吧 ba   particle of suggestion

Interjection (I)

噢 ō/ò   oh (I see)

Idiomatic expressions

请进 qǐng jìn   come in ('please enter')

请问 qǐng wèn   excuse me, (followed by a question)

贵姓 guì xìng   what is your name? (polite:'honourable surname')

Surnames

张 Zhāng

王 Wáng

PRESENTATION

(1) 这是张华同志.
他是中国人.
我们都叫他老张.
老张是北京人.
他爱人姓王,名字叫英英.
我们都叫她小王.
小王是上海人.

(2) 这是张小姐.
那是王先生、王太太.
他们都是华侨.
他们是哪国华侨?
张小姐是英国华侨;
王先生、王太太是美国华侨.

DIALOGUES

(1) 张: 谁啊?
王: 我啊!
张: 你是谁?
王: 我是老王啊.
张: 噢!老王,是你啊,请进.请进!
王: 你们都好吧?
张: 都好.请坐,请坐!
王: 天气真好!
张: 真好,不冷不热!

(2) A: 同志,你姓什么?
B: 我姓张.
A: 叫什么名字?
B: 张华.
A: 张同志什么地方人?
B: 我北京人.
A: 你爱人也是北京人吗?
B: 不是,她是上海人.

(3) A: 请问,您贵姓?
B: 我姓王,我叫王同.您是张同志吧?
A: 是,我叫张华.王先生,您是哪国人?

B: 我是英国人,这是我太太,她是美国人.

A: 王夫人,您好!

C: 您好!张同志是不是上海人?

A: 不是,我是北京人,我爱人是上海人.

(4) A: 你是王同志吧?

B: 不是,我姓张.

A: 噢,张同志,你是不是叫张英?

B: 不是,我名字叫张'京'.

A: 他们都叫你小张吧?

B: 不,他们都叫我老张.

A: 张同志是北京人吧?

B: 不是,我是上海人.

A: 你爱人也是上海人吧?

B: 什么?! 我爱人?! 谁是我爱人?!

SPEECH PATTERNS

(1) Sentences with classificatory verbs

Pattern: Nominal expression (neg) CLV Nominal expression

他　　　　　(不)　是　　英国人　.

1. 他姓王,我不姓王.
2. 他是英国人,你也是英国人吗?
3. 他姓王,名字叫华中.
4. 他是王华中,王先生.

12

(2) Sentences with object and complement

Pattern: S   (neg)   V   O   Complement

他们   (不)   叫   他   小 王.

1. 我们不叫他小王,我们叫他老王.
2. 你们不叫她张小姐吗?   不叫,我们叫她张同志.
3. 他是北京人,我们都叫他'老北京'.
4. 老王真好,我们都叫他好好先生.

(3) Sentences with question words

Pattern: 他是谁?   这是什么?   他是哪国人?

1. 他姓什么?   他姓王.
2. 他叫什么名字?   他叫王华中.
3. 他什么地方人?   他上海人.
4. 张小姐是哪国人?   她是美国人.
5. 她叫张什么?   她叫张美.
6. 她爱人叫王什么中?   他叫王华中.
7. 你们叫他什么?   我们叫他老王.

(4) Sentences with the particle 'ba'

Pattern: Statement   +   <u>ba</u>?

您是中国人   吧?

1. 你们都好吧?   都好,你们呢?
2. 今天不忙吧?   今天不忙,昨天很忙.
3. 他不是美国人吧?   不是,他是英国人.
4. 他们都是华侨吧?   是,他们都是英国华侨.

喝	hē (V) to drink	吃	chī (V) to eat; to take (medicine)
咖	kā * 咖啡 coffee	外	wài * outside, outer, outward; external; foreign
啡	fēi * 咖啡 coffee	菜	cài (N) vegetable; dish (of food); cuisine
只	zhǐ (A) only, merely	学	xué [學] (V) to study, to learn; to imitate
茶	chá (N) tea	话	huà [話] (N) spoken words, speech
看	kàn (V) to look, look at; to see; to visit; to read; to think (have a view)	法	fǎ * method; law Fǎ (or Fà) short for France 法国
电	diàn [電] (N) electricity * electric	德	dé * virtue; morality short for Germany 德国
视	shì [視] (LC) to look at; to regard as; to inspect 电视 television	会	huì [會] (MV) can (know how to) (V) to meet (N) meeting; association
文	wén * writing; language; culture (SV) literary; elegant	说	shuō [說] (V) to speak, to say; to explain; to scold
书	shū [書] (N) book (LC) to write; letter; document	常	cháng (A) often; usually; habitually (AT) ordinary
喜	xǐ * to rejoice; joy	饭	fàn [飯] (N) cooked rice; meal; food
欢	huān * [歡] joyful, merry	应	yǐng * [應] ought to; should; must

14

该	gāi [該] (MV) ought to; should (V) to owe; be sb.'s turn to do sth.	友	yǒu * friend; friendly 朋友 friend
一	yī (NU) one (AT) whole; all; throughout	晚	wǎn (SV) late 晚上 evening
点	diǎn [點] (N) dot; point; speck (V) to dot; to order (a dish)	做	zuò (V) to do; to make (CLV) to be; to act as
儿	ér * [兒] child; non-syllabic diminutive suffix	水	shuǐ (N) water * liquid
想	xiǎng (V) to think, to think (that) (MV) want to, plan to, feel like	谢	xiè [謝] (V) to thank a surname
朋	péng * friend, companion	酒	jiǔ (N) wine, spirits, strong drink

喝	口						
	日						
	匃	ノ	ㄅ	ㄅ	勾	匃	
咖	口	叻	叻	咖			
啡	口	미	미	마	매	啡	啡
只	口	只	只				
茶	艹	一	艹	艹			
	余	ノ	人	今	个	佘	余
看	手	ノ	㇇	三	手		
	目	丨	月	月	目		
电	丶	冂	日	日	电		
视	礻	丶	㇇	礻	礻		
	见	丨	冂	贝	见		
文	丶	亠	六	文			
书	㇇	乛	书	书			
喜	一	十	士	吉	壴	壴	壴 喜
欢	㇇	又	又'	欢	欢		
吃	口	口	叱	吃			
外	ノ	㇁	夕	列	外		
菜	艹	一	艹	艹			
	采	丶	㇛	㇛	㇛	平	采 采
学	𭕄	丶	丷	丷	𭕄		
	子	㇇	了	子			
话	丶	讠	讠	计	计	话	
法	丶	冫	氵	汇	汁	沣	法 法
德	彳	ノ	彳	彳			
	惪	一	十	古	古	南	西 惪 惪

会	ノ	人	厽	今	会	会	
说	丶	讠	讠	讠	讷	说	说
常	𭕄	丨	丷	丷	𭕄		
	口						
	巾	丨	冂	巾			
饭	饣	ノ	㇈	饣			
	反	ノ	厂	厉	反		
应	丶	亠	广	广	应	应	应
该	丶	讠	讠	讠	讠	该	该 该
一	一						
点	丶	十	占	点	点	点	点
儿	ノ	儿					
想	相	一	十	才	木	机	相 相
	心	丶	心	心	心		
朋	ノ	月	月	月	肌	朋	朋
友	一	𠂇	方	友			
晚	日	丨	冂	月	日		
	免	ノ	㇇	夕	刍	召	乸 免
做	亻	ノ	亻				
	古	一	十	古			
	攵	ノ	㇈	𠂆	攵		
水	丨	刂	水	水			
谢	讠		讠				
	身	ノ	亻	亻	竹	身	身 身
	寸	一	寸	寸			
酒	冫	丶	冫				
	酉	一	厂	冂	丙	酉	酉 酉

Verbs (V)

爱 ài   love

喝 hē   drink

看 kàn   look at; read

　看书 kàn-shū (V-O) read

喜欢 xǐhuan   like

吃 chī   eat

　吃饭 chī-fàn (V-O) eat

学 xué   learn

会 huì   know (languages)

说 shuō   say; speak

　说话 shuō-huà (V-O) speak

想 xiǎng   think

做 zuò   do; make

谢谢 xièxie   thank

Modal verbs (MV)

爱 ài   love to, like to , be keen on

喜欢 xǐhuan   like to

会 huì   can; know how to; have capacity for

应该 yīnggāi   should, ought to

想 xiǎng   want to; plan to; feel like

Nouns

咖啡 kāfēi   coffee

茶 chá   tea

电视 diànshì   television

中文 Zhōngwén   Chinese language

文 wén   writing, written word; language

书 shū   book

菜 cài   vegetables; food (not cereals); dish of food

话 huà   speech, spoken words

英文 Yīngwén   English language

法文 Fǎwén   French language

德文 Déwén   German language

饭 fàn   cooked rice or other cereals; meal

(一)点儿 (yì)diǎnr   a little, some

朋友 péngyou   friend

水 shuǐ   water

酒 jiǔ   wine, spirits, strong drink

Adverbs

只 zhǐ   only

常(常) cháng(cháng)   often, habitually

Place words

外国 wàiguó   abroad, foreign parts

法国 Fǎguó   France

德国 Déguó   Germany

Time word

晚上 wǎnshang   evening

Idiomatic expression

谢谢 xièxie   thank you

　　王先生、王太太是英国华侨。王先生爱喝咖啡，王太太不爱喝咖啡，她只爱喝中国茶。王先生爱看电视，王太太不爱看电视，她只爱看中文书。王先生喜欢吃外国菜，王太太不喜欢吃外国菜，她只喜欢吃中国菜。王先生很喜欢学外国话，英文、法文、德文，他都会。王太太不喜欢学外国话，她只会说中国话。她常说："外国人吃外国饭，应该说外国话；中国人吃中国饭，应该说中国话！"

DIALOGUE

王：今天咖啡真好，你也喝一点儿吧！

太：不喝，我这茶很好。

王：看不看电视？

太：不看，我想看点儿书。

王：是英文书吗？

太：不是，是中文书，谁看英文书？！

王：朋友都说你应该学点儿英文。

太：我不学！'外国人说外国话，中国人说中国话'，不是很好吗？！

王：好、好，不学、不学。晚上做点儿法国菜好不好？

太：谁做啊？我不会做法国菜，你想吃你做吧！

(1)

A: 老张,喝不喝茶?

B: 不喝.

A: 喝点儿咖啡吧?

B: 不喝.

A: 水呢?

B: 谢谢你,也不喝.

A: 茶、咖啡、水,都不喝,你想喝什么?

B: 我想喝点儿酒.

(2)

A: 请坐,请坐!今天真冷,喝点儿茶吧!

B: 谢谢,谢谢,这茶真好,是中国茶吧?

A: 是,您常喝中国茶吗?

B: 常喝,我很喜欢喝中国茶.

A: 您也喜欢吃中国菜吗?

B: 很喜欢.

A: 会做不会?

B: 只会吃,不会做!

SPEECH PATTERNS

(1) Sentences with action verbs

Pattern:　　S　(A)　V　　O　　(P)
　　　　　　他　　　看中文书 .

1. 你们喝什么?　　他喝咖啡,我喝茶.
2. 晚上谁做饭?　　我做,你吃不吃?
3. 你不看电视吗?　　不看,我看书.
4. 他喝法国酒,你喝哪国酒?　　我喝德国酒.
5. 他爱人常常做中国菜吗?　　不常做.

(2) Sentences with modal verbs

Pattern:　　S　(A)　MV　V　　O　　(P)

他　　会　说　中国话.

1. 你爱喝茶吗?　　很爱喝.
2. 谁想学中文?　　他想学,我也想学.
3. 我很喜欢吃北京菜,你呢?　　我只喜欢吃上海菜.
4. 你们都会说外国话吗?　　不都会.
5. 我们都应该学做饭吗?　　都应该.

(3) Choice-type questions with objects (or complements)

Pattern:　　S　(MV)　V　O　bu　(MV)　V?

他　　看电视不　看? (=他看不看电视?)

1. 他是北京人不是?　　不是,他是上海人.
2. 他们喝酒不喝?　　不喝,他们都不会喝.
3. 你会做中国菜不会?　　不会(做).
4. 他想学中文不想?　　很想(学).
5. 你喜欢看中文书不喜欢?　　很不喜欢(看).

(4) Sentences with co-ordinated subjects/topics in succession

Pattern: 你、我、他,都不是中国人.

1. 茶、咖啡,都不很热.
2. 法文、德文,他都会说.

3. 中国菜、法国菜,他都不爱吃.

4. 喝法国酒、吃中国菜,谁不喜欢?

5. 他中文书、英文书,都想看.

(5) Co-ordinate clauses with different objects to the same verb

Pattern:　S　V　O_1, yě　V　O_2
　　　　　我　喝　酒,　也　喝　咖啡.

1. 他会说英文,也会说法文.

2. 我想学中文,也想学德文.

3. 他喜欢北京,也喜欢上海.

4. 她常做法国菜,也常做中国菜.

5. 我应该谢谢你,也应该谢谢他.

(6) The use of '(yì)diǎnr'

1. 天气真热,我想喝点儿水.

2. 朋友都说你应该学点儿法文.

3. 你会说中国话吗?　　会(说)一点儿.

4. 请你做点儿上海菜,好不好?

5. 今天晚上你想做什么?　　我想看点儿书.

21

有	yǒu (V) to have; to exist; there is/are	年	nián (N/M) year
位	wèi (M) polite classifier for persons	三	sān (NU) three
普	pǔ * universal; general	十	shí (NU) ten
通	tōng (V) to go through; lead to; have clear passage (SV) passable; logical	二	èr (NU) two
能	néng (MV) can, be capable of	岁	suì [歲] (M) year of age
没	méi [没] (A) not (negator for yǒu 有) * without; -less; un-....-ed	四	sì (NU) four
师	shī [師] (LC) teacher 老师 teacher	个	gè [個] (M) general classifier
两	liǎng [兩] (NU) two (used with measures) a couple of (M) 1/10 of a catty (=50g)	女	nǚ * woman; female; daughter
本	běn (M) volume; copy * root; this, the present	子	zǐ * son; child noun suffix
典	diǎn * record; code; rites; classic 字典 dictionary	因	yīn * cause; because; reason for
汉	hàn * [漢] Han people (Chinese majority race); Han Dynasty; man	为	wèi * [為] for; on account of; for the sake of
就	jiù (A) then; only; right away; just	孩	hái * child 孩子

所	suǒ * 'that which'; place; office; institute (M) for buildings	几	jǐ [幾] (QW) how many ? (small numbers)
以	yǐ * (LC) to take; to use; by; with; by means of 所以 therefore	大	dà (SV) big, large; eldest (child)
总	zǒng * [總] general; in every case; all the time; always	妹	mèi * younger sister 妹妹
累	lèi (SV) tired, weary; fatiguing	知	zhī * to know
要	yào (V) to want; to ask for (MV) want to; be about to, will	道	dào * way; reason; principle; to say; Taoism
多	duō (SV) many, much (A) how (adverb of degree)	妈	mā [媽] (N) mum, mother
可	kě * may, be permitted (A) indeed, certainly	少	shǎo (SV) few, little (V) to lack; to be in want of
父	fù * father	五	wǔ (NU) five
母	mǔ * mother 父母 parents	六	liù (NU) six
定	dìng (V) to fix; to decide on (AT) fixed; settled 一定 definitely, certainly	七	qī (NU) seven
孙	sūn * [孫] grandson 孙子 孙女 granddaughter	八	bā (NU) eight
杯	bēi * cup, glass (M) cup of, glass of	九	jiǔ (NU) nine
共	gòng * together; to share together 一共 altogether; in all		

有	一	ナ	才	冇	有		所	'	ﾉ	ｆ	ｆ ｆ' ｆﾟ ｆﾟ 所
位	亻	仏	伫	位	位		以	ﾉ	ㄴ	以 以	
普	並	ﾟ	丷	广 廿 廿 並 並			总	ﾟ	ㅁ 台 台 总 总		
	日	ﾉ 冂 日 日					累	田	丶 冂 冂 用 田		
通	ﾜ	ﾜ	甬 甬 甬 甬 甬 涌 通				系	糸	く ㄠ ㄠ 糸 糸 系		
能	育	ﾉ ㅿ 广 育 育 育					要	西	一 冂 冂 两 两 西		
	匕	ﾉ 匕 匕 匕					女	く 女 女			
没	氵	氵 氵 沪 沪 没					多	ﾉ ㄅ 夕 多 多 多			
师	丨	ﾘ 沪 师 师 师					可	一 口 可			
两	一	厂 丙 丙 两 两					父	' 八 父 父			
本	一	十 才 木 本					母	乚 母 母 母 母			
典	丶 冂 冂 由 曲 典 典						定	丶 丶 宀 宀 宁 宁 定 定			
汉	氵 汀 汉						孙	ㄱ 了 子 孑 孙 孙			
就	京	亠 亠 亠 京 京					杯	一 十 才 木 杧 朴 杯 杯			
	尤	一 ナ 尢 尤					共	一 十 廿 共 共 共			
年	ﾉ 广 ㄠ 广 左 年						几	ﾉ 几			
三	一 三 三						大	一 ナ 大			
十	一 十						妹	く 女 女 妌 妌 妹 妹			
二	一 二						知	ﾉ 广 乍 矢 矢 知			
岁	丨 山 少 岁 岁						道	首 丶 丷 广 产 首 首 首			
四	丶 冂 冂 四 四							辶 丶 辶 辶			
个	ﾉ 人 个						妈	く 女 女 妇 妈 妈			
女	く 女 女						少	丨 小 小 少			
子	ㄱ 了 子						五	一 丁 五 五			
因	丨 冂 冂 因 因						六	丶 亠 亠 六			
为	丶 ﾉ 为 为						七	一 七 七			
孩	子 ㄱ 了 孑						八	ﾉ 八			
	亥	亠 亠 亥 亥 亥					九	ﾉ 九			

24

VOCABULARY

Numbers (NU)

一 yī one (2nd tone before 4th, 4th tone before 1, 2, 3)

二 èr two

两 liǎng two (used with measures), a couple of

三 sān three

四 sì four

五 wǔ five

六 liù six

七 qī seven

八 bā eight } optionally 2nd tone before 4th tone

九 jiǔ nine

十 shí ten

Measures (M)

位 wèi polite classifier for persons

本 běn classifier for books

年 nián year

岁 suì year of age

个 gè general classifier

杯 bēi cup of, glass of

天 tiān day

Nouns

普通话 pǔtōnghuà common language, lingua franca, Mandarin

老师 lǎoshī teacher

字典 zìdiǎn dictionary

汉 Hàn Han dynasty; majority people in China; Chinese(in certain combinations)

女儿 nǚ'ér daughter

儿子 érzi son

孩子 háizi child

父母 fùmǔ father and mother

孙子 sūnzi grandson

妹妹 mèimei younger sister

妈 mā mum, mother (familiar)

Stative verbs

普通 pǔtōng common, ordinary

累 lèi tired, weary; fatiguing

多 duō many, much

大 dà big, large; eldest (child)

少 shǎo few, little

Verbs

有 yǒu have; exist; there is/are

生 shēng give birth to, produce; be born

想要 xiǎngyào desire

要 yào want; ask for

知道 zhīdao know

Movable adverbs (MA)

因为 yīnwei because

所以 suǒyǐ therefore

为什么 wèishenme why (because of what?)

可是 kěshi but

一共 yígòng altogether

Modal verbs

能 néng can, be capable of

要 yào want to; be about to, will

Adverbs

没 méi negator for 'yǒu' 有

就(是) jiù(shi) be precisely, exactly, indeed

总(是) zǒng(shi) always

这么 zhème so (this-wise); also pron. 'zème'

那么 nàme so (that-wise); also pron. 'nème'

一定 yídìng definitely, certainly

太 tài too, excessively

Time word

今年 jīnnián this year

Question words

几 jǐ how many (small numbers)

多少 duōshao how many

Measures

个： 一个人； 两个朋友； 三个地方； 四个孩子； 五个什么？

位： 六位朋友；七位老师；八位华侨；九位同志； 几位小姐？

本： 九本书； 十本字典

杯： 两杯茶； 一杯咖啡； 三杯酒

岁： 七十岁

年： 二十五年

天： 十四天

PRESENTATION

　　我有一位朋友姓王,是上海人,我们都叫他小王.小王会说上海话,也会说普通话;能看中文书,也能看英文书.他学英文没有老师,只有两本字典:一本英汉字典,一本汉英字典.他说这两本字典就是两位老师.小王今年三十二岁,有四个女儿,没有儿子.因为这四个孩子都很小,所以他总是很忙,很累.有一位朋友问他为什么要生这么多孩子,是不是因为想要个儿子?小王说:"我不想要儿子,可是我父母一定要个孙子!"

DIALOGUE

A: 真累,真累!

B: 喝杯茶吧,是不是因为天气太热?

A: 不是,是因为孩子太多.

B: 你一共有几个?

A: 四个,都是女儿.

B: 为什么要生那么多?是不是想要个儿子?

A: 我们不想要儿子,可是我父母一定要个孙子!

B: 这个是你大女儿吧?今年几岁?

C: 我五岁.

B: 你有几个妹妹?

C: 不知道.

B: 不知道?!为什么?

C: 我妈常常生妹妹,我也不知道她一共要生几个.

(1)

A: 一共有多少? 很多吧?

B: 一、二、三、四、五、六、七......

A: 有没有四十个?

B: 不知道。八、九、十、十一、十二......

A: 我们一个人有几个?

B: 你能不能不说话? 十三、十四、十五......一共二十七个。

A: 什么?! 只有二十七个?! 这么少?!

B: 我们九个人,三九、二十七,一个人三个,不多也不少!

(2)

A: 你知道那两个人是谁吗?

B: 哪两个?

A: 那两个,你看! 就是那两个外国人。

B: 噢,他们啊,一位是我们法文老师,一位是我们德文老师。

A: 他们两位都会说中国话吗?

B: 都会。他们总是说中国话,很少说法文,也很少说德文。

A: 为什么?

B: 因为法文老师不会说德文,德文老师也不会说法文。

SPEECH PATTERNS

(1) Quantification of nouns

Pattern:　　Number　Measure　Noun
　　　　　　　三　　　个　　　人

1. 他有两个中国朋友,都姓王.

2. 你要几本字典? 三本.

3. 他们有几个孩子? 两个,一个七岁,一个九岁.

4. 他们要多少本? 六十本.

5. 我想喝杯茶. 请坐,请坐!

6. 你们有多少人? 四十八个.

7. 一共多少天? 十五天.

(2) Specification of nouns

Patterns: SP NU M N

a. 这 茶

b. 这 (一) 杯 茶

c. 那 三 杯 咖啡

1. 这茶很好。(Contrast: 谁要喝这杯茶?)

2. 那本字典不是汉英字典,你有汉英字典没有?
   我没有,他有一本.

3. 这个人说这个好,那个人说那个好;你说哪个好?
   这个,那个,都不好.

4. 我很喜欢那两本书,你呢? 哪两本书?

5. 这两杯酒,一杯你喝,一杯我喝,好不好?
   我不会喝,都请你喝吧.

6. 你那四位朋友都会说普通话吗? 两个会,两个不会.

(3) Indirect questions

1. 他问我谁有字典.

2. 我问他老王会说英文不会,他说不知道.

3. 他不知道哪位是王老师.

4. 我问他那是什么,他说(那)是电视.

5. 你知道她为什么要生这么多孩子吗?

6. 她不说她是哪国人,所以我们不知道她是哪国人.

(4) <u>Sentences with the pivotal construction</u>

Pattern:	Sub	Verb	Obj Sub	Verb	(Obj)	
	谁	请	我	喝	茶	?
	我	有个朋友	姓	王		.

1. 他问我会不会说普通话.

   (Contrast: 他问我小王会不会说普通话.)

2. 我有个朋友叫老王,他有个女儿总是喜欢说话.

3. 今天晚上他们要请我吃德国菜.

4. 有人说他有九个儿子,八十一个孙子.　谁?

5. 他常说没有人不喜欢吃中国菜,可是我就不喜欢.

家	jiā (N) home; family * a specialist in a certain field	还	hái [還] (A) still, yet; in addition
客	kè (N) guest, visitor	汤	tāng [湯] (N) soup a surname
李	lǐ * plum 李子 a common surname	瓶	píng * vase, bottle, glass jar (M) bottle of, vase of
口	kǒu (N) mouth; opening (M) for members of family; wells	钱	qián [錢] (N) money a surname
跟	gēn (C) and (CV) with; along with (V) to follow	够	gòu [夠] (SV) enough, sufficient (A) quite, pretty; enough to
的	de (K) marker of subordination	肯	kěn (MV) be willing to, agree to
买	mǎi [買] (V) to buy	行	xíng (SV) pass muster; be OK (LC) to walk; to carry out

只	zhī [隻]
	(M) for birds and some anim-
	  al (among other things);
	  one of a pair
		半	bàn
			(NU/M) half; half of
			一半 (a) half
			半个 half (of)...

鸡	jī [雞] (N) chicken	准	zhǔn (V) to allow; to be allowed
条	tiáo [條] (M) for fish and various long narrow things	怎	zěn * 怎么 how (in what manner); how come? what?
鱼	yú [魚] (N) fish	样	yàng * [樣] manner; shape (M) kind, type
青	qīng * blue or green 青天 blue sky 青菜 green vegetables	抽	chōu (V) to draw out; to smoke (cigarettes,etc.)

支	zhī (M) for pens, cigarettes, etc. +	笔	bǐ [筆] (N) pen (M) stroke; sum of money

烟	yān
	(N) smoke; cigarette,
	  tobacco
		用	yòng
			(V) to use; to employ
			(CV) using, by means of,
			  with

包	bāo
	(V) to wrap
	(M) a package, packet
		份	fèn
			(M) a share; portion; copy (
			  of newspaper, magazine,
			  document, etc.)

对	duì [對] (CV) to(wards) (SV) correct; that's right (M) pair of	报	bào [報] (V) to report; to requite (N) newspaper; bulletin; report
起	qǐ * [起] to rise, to raise, to begin		

+ 枝 is also used for pens, cigarettes, etc.

家	宀	丶 宀 宀
	豕	一 丆 丆 丂 豖 豕 豖
客	宀	丶 宀 宀
	各	丿 久 冬 各
李		一 十 才 木 杏 李 李
口		丶 冂 口
跟	足	口 巳 巳 呈 足
	艮	丁 彐 艮 艮 艮
的		丿 亻 亻 白 白 白' 的 的
买		一 フ ヲ �买 买
只		口 尸 只
鸡	又	フ 又
	鸟	丿 勹 勺 鸟 鸟
条		丿 久 久 冬 夅 条
鱼		丿 久 勺 勹 甬 鱼 鱼
青		一 二 丰 主 丰 青 青 青
还		一 丆 丆 不 不 还 还
汤		氵 汀 汤 汤
瓶	并	丶 丷 丷 兰 并 并
	瓦	一 乙 瓦 瓦
钱	钅	丿 卜 卜 乍 钅
	戋	一 二 戋 戋 戋

够	句	丿 勹 句
	多	丿 夕 夕 多 多 多
肯		丨 卜 止 止 片 肯 肯 肯
行		丿 彳 彳 彳 行 行
半		丶 丷 丷 兰 半
准		冫 冫 冫 冫 汁 件 准 准 准
怎		丿 亻 午 乍 乍 乍 怎 怎 怎
样		一 十 才 木 木 栏 栏 栏 样
抽		一 十 才 扣 扣 抽 抽
支		一 十 キ 支
烟	火	丶 丷 少 火 丿 丷 少 火
	因	丨 冂 尸 团 团 因
包		丿 勹 勺 包
对		フ 又 対 对
起	走	一 十 土 丰 丰 走 走
	己	フ コ 己
笔	竹	丿 竹 竹 竹 竹 竹
	毛	丿 二 三 毛
用		丿 冂 月 月 用
份		亻 亻 仏 份 份
报		一 十 才 护 护 报 报

VOCABULARY

家 jiā (N) family; home

客人 kèren (N) guest

请 qǐng (V) invite

李 Lǐ (surname)

口 kǒu (M) measure for members of
    family
    (N) mouth

跟 gēn (C) and
    (CV) along with

同学 tóngxué (N) fellow-student (can
    be used as title)

的 de (K) marker of subordination

买 mǎi (V) buy

只 zhī (M) measure for birds and
    some animals (among
    other things)

鸡 jī (N) chicken

条 tiáo (M) measure for fish and
    various long narrow
    things

鱼 yú (N) fish

青菜 qīngcài (N) green vegetables

还(是) hái(shi) in addition; still,
    yet

汤 tāng (N) soup

瓶 píng (M) bottle of, vase of

钱 qián (N) money

够 gòu (SV) enough

肯 kěn (MV) be willing to, agree to

行 xíng (SV) pass muster, be OK

半 bàn (NU/M) half; half of

可以 kěyǐ (MV) be permissible;
    can, may

准 zhǔn (V) allow, be allowed

怎么样 zěnmeyàng (IE) what's it
    like? how's things? what
    do you think? Well then...

贵 guì (SV) dear, expensive

那么 nàme (IE) in that case

抽 chōu (V) draw out; smoke (
    cigarettes, etc.)

烟 yān (N) smoke; cigarette, tabacco

抽烟 chōu-yān (V-O) smoke

支 zhī (M) for pens, cigarettes, etc.

包 bāo (M) a package, packet

对不起 duìbuqǐ (IE) sorry, pardon
    me, excuse me

字 zì (N) written character,
    (monosyllabic) word

对 duì (SV) correct; that's right

先 xiān (A) first, in advance,
    before

笔 bǐ (N) pen

用 yòng (V) use
    (CV) using, by means of,
    with

份 fèn (M) copy (of newspaper,
    magazine, etc.)

报 bào (N) newspaper, report
    (V) to report

老张家今天晚上有客人.他们请谁?他们请老李家.李家一共有五口儿人:老李,他爱人跟三个孩子.老张跟老李是老同学,也是很好的朋友.他们两家的孩子也都是好朋友.老张的爱人今天想买一只鸡、一条鱼、跟一点儿青菜.她要做四个菜,两个冷的,两个热的,还要做一个汤.老张很喜欢喝酒,他请他爱人买两瓶.他爱人说钱不够,不肯买.老张说请人吃饭没酒不行,问他爱人买半条鱼,买一瓶酒,可不可以.他爱人说:"好吧,我买一瓶,可是晚上你不准吃鱼!"

DIALOGUE

张: 怎么样,今天想买点儿什么菜?

爱: 我想买一只鸡、一条鱼跟一点儿青菜;四个菜一个汤,怎么样?

张: 好啊,几个冷的,几个热的?

爱: 两个冷的,两个热的.

张: 酒呢?

爱: 老李跟他爱人都不会喝酒,买酒谁喝?

张: 请人吃饭,不能没酒,买两瓶吧!

爱: 酒那么贵,我的钱不够.

张: 钱不够?! 不买鱼行不行?

爱: 两家的孩子都爱吃鱼,没鱼不行!

张: 那么,买半条鱼,买一瓶酒,可不可以?

爱: 好吧,我买一瓶,可是晚上你不准吃鱼!

SKETCHES

(1)

A: 怎么样,忙吗?抽支烟吧.我这包是法国烟.

B: 抽烟?! 对不起,请你看看那四个大字.

A: 什么?!"不准抽烟"!

B: 对!这个地方不准抽烟,你看看书吧.

A: 那本书是谁的?我看看可以吗?

B: 哪本?是这本小书吗?

A: 不是,是那本大的.

B: 那是老张的,你先问问他吧.

A: 这支笔是你的吧?我用用可以吗?

B: 笔也是老张的.

A: 这份报也是他的吗?

B: 报是我的,你看吧! —— 是昨天的.

(2)

A: 李先生,那位是......

B: 那位啊,他是我朋友钱汉.

A: 噢!他就是钱汉啊!你们是老朋友吧?

B: 是啊,我们是三十年的老朋友.

A: 钱先生总是那么忙吗?

B: 他总是那么忙,所以我们都叫他大忙人.

A: 有人说他不喝酒,可是你看......

B: 噢!你不知道啊?!他不喝酒是不肯喝普通的酒,今天的
酒这么好,他还肯不喝吗?

SPEECH PATTERNS

(1) Nouns modified by other nouns

(a) more often without de

Pattern:　　N　　　　N

我　妹妹不喜欢做饭。

1. 他太太总是说钱不够。
2. 老张家一共有八口儿人。
3. 他会说中国话,也能看中文报。
4. 上海人都爱吃鱼吗?
5. 他爱人不准他喝外国酒,也不准他抽外国烟。
6. 今天没有鸡汤,青菜汤行不行?　　青菜汤我不喝。

(b) usually with de

Pattern:　　　N　de　N

我妹妹的爱人很喜欢做饭。

1. 老王的太太总是说钱不够。
2. 我跟他是二十年的老朋友,可是不知道他是什么地方人。
3. 这是今天的报吧,我看看可以吗?
4. 那不是他们家的孩子,那是他们家客人的孩子。
5a. 老张家的那两个孩子都很好。
 b. 老张家那两个孩子的名字都很好。

(c) where the modified noun is understood

Pattern:　这杯咖啡是谁的?

1. 哪包是你的?
  这包是我的,那包也是我的,这两包都是我的。
2. 那两只鸡都是他们的吗?　　都是。

3. 这半瓶酒不是你的吧？　　不是,是我同学老王的。

4. 这份报是今天的不是？　　不是,是昨天的。

5. 对不起,这个是我的。　　你的？谁说是你的？

(2) Nouns modified by stative verbs

(a) more often without de

Pattern:

他有一个 小 电视.

（SV N）

1. 他们冷天喝咖啡,热天喝茶。

2. 大鱼吃小鱼,小鱼吃什么？

3. 他没有很多钱,可是还要喝好酒,抽好烟。

4. 好人很少,好书也不多,这话对不对？　　很对。

(b) usually with de

Pattern:

他有一个很小的电视.

（SV de N）

1. 这是一本很普通的书,为什么不准我看？

2. 为什么他们都想抽那么贵的烟？

3. 我不知道他们两个人是很好的朋友。

4. 他想买一支不太贵的笔。

(c) where the modified noun is understood

Pattern: 大的是我的,小的是他的。

1. 想喝什么？冷的也有,热的也有。　　我想先喝杯茶。

2. 好的是他的,不好的也是他的。

3. 这个是贵的,贵的不一定好。

4. 王家的两个女儿,大的八岁,小的六岁。

5. 他们家老的、小的，一共十二口儿人。

1. 晚上想做什么？   想看看电视。
2. 这是什么鱼？   我也不知道，问问老张吧。
3. 对不起，我想问问您这个中国话叫什么？
   中国话叫'字典'.
4. 你会做中国菜吗？   不会，可是很想学学。
5. 你为什么要请他吃饭？   他常常请我，我也应该请请他。
6. 你请我喝酒，我应该谢谢你。   不谢，不谢。

Patterns: a. 我可(以)不可以吃鱼？
         b. 我可以吃鱼不可以？

1. 你喜不喜欢喝咖啡？   很喜欢。
2. 他应不应该喝那么多酒？   很不应该。
3. 我可不可以看看您的报？   可以可以。
4. 我问他喜不喜欢这个地方，他不肯说。

明	míng * bright; clear 明天 tomorrow Ming the Ming dynasty	新	xīn (SV) new; fresh; up-to-date
日	rì * the sun; day; day of the month	闻	wén [聞] (LC) to hear (V) to smell a surname
东	dōng [東] (L) east	乐	yuè * [樂] music 音乐 a surname
西	xī (L) west 东西 thing (object, article)	现	xiàn * [現] present; current; existing; to manifest
给	gěi [給] (V) to give (CV) to; for	在	zài (V) to exist; to be in, at; to be living (CV) in; at
容	róng * to contain a surname	件	jiàn (M) piece, item
易	yì * easy; to change a surname	毛	máo (M) 1/10 of <u>yuán</u> 元 (N) fur; hair (of body) a surname
送	sòng (V) to give as a present; to deliver; to see sb. off	衣	yī * clothes

收	shōu
	 (V) to receive; to collect;
	     to put away
		得	děi
			 (MV) have to, must; need to
			 (V) to cost (money), take (
			     time)

音	yīn * sound (N) sound (in phonetics)	块	kuài [塊] (M) unit of currency; lump; piece
机	jī * [機] machine; mechanism; opportunity	便	pián * 便宜 cheap
听	tīng [聽] (V) to listen to; to hear; to obey	宜	yí * suitable; appropriate

事	shì (N) matter; job	苹	píng * [蘋] 苹果 apple
情	qíng * feeling; affection; emotion; situation; condition	果	guǒ * fruit; result, outcome
当	dāng [當] * ought to, should (CLV) to be (in the role of), serve as	卖	mài [賣] (V) to sell

然	rán
	(LC) so, thus; right, correct;
	     but, nevertheless
	当然 of course
		斤	jīn
			(M) catty (500 gr.)
			   1 斤 = 10 两

难	nán [難] (SV) difficult	坏	huài [壞] (SV) bad; spoiled; out of order
时	shí * [時] time 小时 hour	零	líng (NU) zero, nil (AT) odd, spare
间	jiān [間] * between; among (M) for rooms 时间 time, length of time	民	mín * the people; of the people; folk; civilian

念	niàn
	(V) to read books; to read
	     aloud; to study an aca-
	     demic subject
		币	bì * [幣]
			currency
			人民币 Renminbi (RMB)

去	qù (V) to go (to) * of last year 去年	元	yuán (M) basic unit of currency 1 元 = 10 角 = 100 分
图	tú [圖] (N) diagram; drawing; chart; map * picture	角	jiǎo [角] (M) 1/10 of yuán (written)

种	zhǒng [種]
	(M) kind, sort, type;
	     species
		分	fēn
			(M) 1/100 of yuán, cent;
			     minute (1/60 of an hour)
			(V) to divide

找	zhǎo (V) to look for; to seek; to give as change		

明	丶	刀	日	日	明	明	明	明
日	丨	刀	日	日
东	一	七	左	东	东
西	一	匸	襾	两	两	西
给	纟	幺	纟	纟
合	丶	人	合	合
容	丶	丷	宀	宀	宛	突	容
易	丶	冂	日	日	月	昜	易
送	丷	丷	芏	羊	关	关	送	送
收	レ	丩	丩	收	收	收
音	丶	二	立	立	音
机	一	十	才	木	机	机
听	口	口	听	听	听
新	亲	丶	一	立	立	辛	辛	亲
	斤	丿	斤	斤	斤
闻	丶	丨	门	门	闫	闻	闻	闻
乐	丿	二	千	乐	乐
现	一	二	干	王	玑	玑	现	现
在	一	ナ	才	右	在	在
件	亻	亻	亻	仁	件
毛	丿	二	三	毛
衣	丶	一	亠	才	衣	衣
得	彳	彳	彳	得	得	得	得	得
块	一	十	土	圤	圹	块
便	亻	亻	伊	伊	佰	便	便

宜	丶	丷	宀	广	市	审	宜	宜
事	一	匚	写	写	写	写	事
情	丨	忄	忄	忄	忄	忭	忭	情	情
当	丨	丷	丷	当	当
然	丿	夕	夕	夕	外	外	然	然	然	然
难	丆	叉	叉	对	对	𪣻	难	难	难
时	日	旪	时	时
间	丶	冂	门	间
念	丿	人	亽	今	念	念	念
去	一	十	土	去	去
图	丨	门	冈	冈	冈	冈	图	图
种	丿	二	千	禾	禾	和	和	种
找	一	十	扌	扒	找	找
苹	一	十	卝	艹	苎	荁	苹	苹
果	丶	冂	日	旦	甲	果	果
卖	一	十	土	吉	吉	古	卖	卖
斤	丿	斤	斤	斤
坏	一	十	土	圹	圷	坏
零	雨	一	一	雨	雨	零	零	零
令	丿	人	亽	今	令
民	𠃌	口	尸	民	民
币	丶	亻	币	币
元	一	二	亓	元
角	丿	冖	产	介	角	角	角
分	丿	八	分	分

42

VOCABULARY

明天 míngtiān (TW) tomorrow

生日 shēngrì (N) birthday

东西 dōngxi (N) thing (object, article)

给 gěi (V) give

容易 róngyì (SV) easy

送 sòng (V) give (as present); send, deliver; see sb. off

收音机 shōuyīnjī (N) radio receiver

听 tīng (V) listen to

新闻 xīnwén (N) news

音乐 yīnyuè (N) music

现在 xiànzài (TW) now

件 jiàn (M) piece, item

毛衣 máoyī (N) sweater, woolly

得 děi (MV) must; need to (V) cost (money); take (time)

块 kuài (M) unit of currency (wr. yuán 元); piece; lump

便宜 piányi (SV) cheap

事情 shìqing (N) matter; job

当然 dāngrán (MA) of course

就 jiù (A) then (introduces a consequence or conclusion)

难 nán (SV) difficult

有用 yǒu-yòng (SV) useful (lit: have use)

要是 yàoshi (MA) if

天天 tiāntiān (TW) day after day; everyday

时间 shíjiān (N) time

念 niàn (V) read (aloud); study an academic subject

念书 niàn-shū (V-O) study (read books)

去年 qùnián (TW) last year

地图 dìtú (N) map, atlas

种 zhǒng (M) kind, sort, type

毛 máo (M) 1/10 of yuán 元 (wr. jiǎo 角)

找 zhǎo (V) look for; give as change

苹果 píngguǒ (N) apple

怎么 zěnme (QW) how? what?

卖 mài (V) sell

斤 jīn (M) catty (500 gr.)

坏 huài (SV) bad

水果 shuǐguǒ (N) fruit

两 liǎng (M) unit of weight (=50 gr.)

零 líng (NU) zero, nil

零钱 língqián (N) change, odd coins

张 zhāng (M) sheet of

人民币 Rénmínbì (N) 'People's Currency'

人民 rénmín (N) the people

元 yuán (M) basic unit of currency

角 jiǎo (M) 1/10 of yuán 元 (written)

分 fēn (M) 1/100 of yuán 元, cent

PRESENTATION

明天是我们家老二的生日,我们想买个东西给他.老二今年十五岁,买东西给他真不容易:他喜欢的,我们不想给;我们想给的,他不一定喜欢.今年我说送他一个小收音机,可以听听新闻,也可以听听音乐.我太太说收音机太贵,现在天气这么冷,应该送他一件毛衣.收音机是很贵,得三十块钱,可是毛衣也不便宜,好的也要二十多.我们家的事情,大的听我的,小的听我太太的;买孩子的东西当然是小事,太太说买毛衣就买毛衣吧!

DIALOGUE

A:　明天老二生日,你说买什么给他?

B:　买东西给他真难!

A:　是不容易!他喜欢的,我们不想给;我们想给的,他不一定喜欢.

B:　买个小收音机给他,怎么样?

A:　收音机太贵,我想得三十块吧!

B:　收音机是不便宜,可是很有用:可以听新闻,也可以听音乐.

A:　要是他天天听音乐,还有时间念书吗?

B:　那么你说买什么呢?

A:　买件毛衣吧.

B:　我们去年给他的不也是毛衣吗?

A:　去年是去年,今年是今年.现在天气这么冷,一件毛衣够吗?

B:　当然不够!好好好,你说买毛衣就买毛衣吧!

(1) A: 您要买什么?

B: 我这两个孩子,老大要买一本英汉字典,老二要买一本地图.

A: 我们有两种英汉字典:这种小的七块半,那种大的十二块.

B: 看看可以吗?

A: 当然可以.

B: 大的字多,就买大的吧.

A: 好,您还要买地图是不是?这本怎么样?只要六块三毛五.

B: 老二,你看看,行不行?

C: 行,我们老师用的就是这种.

B: 好,就买这本,一共多少钱?

A: 字典十二块,地图六块三毛五,一共十八块三毛五.

B: 一五、一十、十五、二十,给你二十块.

A: 谢谢,找您一块六毛五.

(2) A: 苹果怎么卖?

B: 四毛五一斤,两斤八毛,您要几斤?

A: 一斤有几个?

B: 大的一斤只有四个,小的有五个.

A: 我买两斤吧,坏的不要.

B: 我们卖的水果没有坏的,个个儿都好,两斤二两行不行?

A: 行,多少钱?

B: 八毛五.

A: 我没零钱,给你一张五块的行吗?

B: 行,找您四块一毛五,再见!

A: 再见!

SPEECH PATTERNS

(1) Units of currency

RMB 人民币	Spoken	Written	
Basic unit (yuán) 1/10 yuán 1/100 yuán	块 毛 分	元 角 分	
		(a)	(b)
RMB ¥ 0.05	五分(钱)	五分	0.05
0.10	一毛(钱)	一角	0.10
0.85	八毛五(分)	八角五分	0.85
1.00	一块(钱)	一元	1.00
1.20	一块二(毛)/一块两毛	一元二角	1.20
2.50	两块半/两块五(毛)	二元五角	2.50
4.73	四块七毛三(分)	四元七角三分	4.73
10.06	十块零 六分	十元零 六分	10.06
10.50	十块半/十块五毛	十元五角	10.50
37.41	三十七块四毛一(分)	三十七元四角一分	37.41
90.05	九十块零 五分	九十元零 五分	90.05

Stamps: 5分; 10分; 20分; 50分; 70分

(2) Asking prices (Amount per unit)

(a) 这本书(卖/要)多少钱?/几块钱?/几毛钱?/几分钱?

(b) 苹果多少钱一斤?/苹果一斤多少钱?/一斤苹果多少钱?

(c) 这种烟多少钱一包?/这种烟一包多少钱?

(d) 苹果怎么卖? 1. 一斤四毛五./四毛五一斤.

2. 一个一毛./一毛一个.

46

酒怎么卖？　1. 五块半一瓶. / 一瓶五块半.
　　　　　　2. 两毛二一杯. / 一杯两毛二.

鱼怎么卖？　1. 一条五毛. / 五毛一条.
　　　　　　2. 一斤八毛四 / 八毛四一斤.

(3) <u>Goods at certain prices (noun constructions)</u>

1a. 两块钱的苹果.

　b. 两块钱一斤的苹果.

2a. 八块钱的酒.

　b. 八块钱一瓶的酒.

3. 一块钱一只的鸡.

4. 一毛钱一杯的茶.

5. 七毛五一包的烟.

(4) <u>'Duō' and 'bàn'</u>

(a) <u>duō</u>

1. NU – M – <u>duō</u>

(a) 一个多 (苹果)

(b) 两岁多

(c) 三杯多 (酒)

(d) 四毛多 (钱)

(e) 五块多 (钱)

(f) 五十五块多

2. NU – <u>duō</u> – M

(a) 二十多位 (客人)

(b) 三十多件 (毛衣)

(c) 十多本 (地图)

(d) 八十多支 (笔)

(b) <u>bàn</u>

1. <u>bàn</u> – M

(a) 半瓶酒

(b) 半条鱼

(c) 半斤水果

(d) 三个半条鱼

2. NU – M – <u>bàn</u>

(a) 三只半 (鸡)

(b) 四个半

(c) 五岁半

(d) 六斤半 (苹果)

(e) 七块半 (钱)

(f) 九十五块半

3. <u>yí bàn</u>

(a) 他的书,一半是英文的。

(b) 吃饭的钱,一人给一半。

(c) 他买的那五十个苹果,一半不能吃。

(5) <u>Sentences with both direct and indirect objects</u>

Pattern:　　　S　　V indO　　dirO
我 想 送 他 一点儿东西。

1. 他只肯给我两毛钱。

2. 她没有收音机,我们送她一个收音机怎么样?

3. 你想不想给他那么多呢?　　我只想给他一半。

4. 你说送他什么呢?　　送他两包烟吧。

5. 要是他不给我们东西,我们就不给他钱。

(6) <u>Modification of nouns by clauses with 'de'</u>

(a) Pattern:　　S　(MV)　V　<u>de</u>　N
他　　喜欢 的 东 西 都很贵。

1. 你知道的(事情)真多。

2. 我看的这三本书都是老王的。

3. 我们都爱吃她做的鱼。

4. 他要找的(东西)不是这个。

5. 你说的是中国话吗?

6. 他说的那种事(情)没人爱听。

(b) Pattern:　　(MV) V　　O　　<u>de</u>　　N
会 说 中国话 的 英国人多不多?

1. 爱喝酒的人一定没钱。

2. 看报的那个人是我朋友.

3. 喜欢听音乐的人都知道那个地方.

4. 卖书的那位老先生总是没时间做他喜欢做的事.

5. 为什么买东西的人这么多? 这个地方的东西便宜.

6. 不看报的人当然不知道这条新闻.

(c) Pattern:　　 S　　　 V　 ind O　 _de_　　 N

我们去年给　他　的　东西也是毛衣.

1. 他不太喜欢吃我们给他的那种水果.

2. 他们送我的东西没有好的.

3. 这是他给你的钱吧? 你怎么知道?

4. 你昨天问我的话,我现在可以问他吗? 当然可以.

5. 老师给我们的书就是这本.

(d) Clausal expressions which have become independent nouns

1. 卖报的　　　　　　　　4. 要饭的

2. 送报的　　　　　　　　5. 卖鱼的

3. 做饭的　　　　　　　　6. 报新闻的

(7) Reduplication of measure words

1. 他天天晚上都要喝两杯.

2. 我买的苹果个个儿都是坏的.

3. 他们年年儿都要送我一瓶酒.

4. 这个地方家家都有电视.

5. 老张那五个孩子,个个儿会做饭.

6. 学中文的人天天晚上都得念书.

49

前	qián (L) front, front of *before; ago; former	打	dǎ (V) to hit; to fight; to play (cards and some ball games)
胖	pàng (SV) fat (of persons)	极	jí [極] *the utmost point; extreme (A) extremely, exceedingly
了	le (P) modal particle indica- ting change of state	拳	quán (N) fist (M) for a punch 打拳 (V-O) to box
觉	jué * [覺] to sense, to feel; to find that; to become aware	形	xíng * shape, form
得	dé (V) to get; to receive (K) complement marker	完	wán (V) to finish * to be over; whole
每	měi (SP) each, every	全	quán [全] (SV) complete; whole; entire
睡	shuì (V) to sleep	瘦	shòu (SV) thin, slim; lean; tight (of clothes)
觉	jiào [覺] (N/M) a nap, a sleep 睡觉 (V-O) to sleep	精	jīng * essence; refined; skilled spirit
别	bié [別] (SP) other; different (A) = 不要 don't...(in imper- ative sentences)	神	shén (N) god; deity * spirit; mind
后	hòu [後] (L) back, behind, rear * after; later; afterwards	工	gōng (N) work; labour
来	lái [來] (V) to come; pro-verb stand- ing for other verbs in context:我不会,请你来吧!	作	zuò (V) to do; to make; to write; to compose
教	jiāo (V) to teach, to instruct 教书 (V-O) to teach	顿	dùn [頓] (M) for meals; bout of

碗	wǎn (N) bowl (M) bowl of	怕	pà (V) to fear, to dread; to be 　　afraid that
饿	è　　　　　　[餓] (SV) hungry (V) to starve	欸	ê̄, ēi, āi (I) hey! oi!
饱	bǎo　　　　　[飽] (SV) be full, replete	认	rèn　　　*　[認] to recognize; to acknowledge; to admit; to identify
虽	suī　　　*　[雖] although 虽然	识	shí　　　*　[識] to know; to recognize; knowledge
敢	gǎn　　　　　[敢] (MV) dare to	亲	qīn　　　　　[親] * closely related; relative; 　intimate (V) to kiss
公	gōng　　　　* public; equitable; male (of animals); metric: 公斤 kilo	身	shēn　　　* body; oneself, itself
恐	kǒng　　　* afraid; fear; terrify	体	tǐ　　　　*　[體] body; style; form; system

前	`` 丷 丷 兰 广 芦 肯 首 前 前 ``	神 ` 丶 ㇆ 礻 礻 初 袒 袒 神
胖	丿 月 月 月 胖 胖 胖 胖	工 一 丁 工
了	㇇ 了	作 亻 伫 仁 作 作 作
觉	丶 丷 丷 灬 ⺍ 兴 ⺍ 觉 觉	顿 屯 一 匚 凵 屯
得	彳 得 得 得 得 得	页 一 丆 丆 万 页 页
每	丿 亠 乞 乞 每 每 每	碗 石 一 丆 石
睡	目 丨 冂 冃 目	宛 丶 丷 宀 宀 宎 宛 宛
垂	丿 二 三 幺 幺 幺 垂 垂	饿 饣 丿 亇 饣
别	口 号 另 别 别	我 丿 亠 于 扌 我 我 我
后	丿 厂 斤 后	饱 饣 丿 亇 饣
来	一 ㇇ 冂 亚 束 来 来	包 丿 勹 匀 包
教	孝 一 十 土 耂 耂 孝	虽 口 吕 吊 虽 虽
	攵 丿 亻 ケ 攵	敢 耳 一 工 尸 开 开 耳 耳
打	一 十 扌 扩 打	攵 丿 亻 ケ 攵
极	一 十 才 木 朾 极 极	公 丿 八 公 公
拳	类 丶 丷 ⺍ 兰 半 类	恐 一 丁 工 玑 巩 巩 恐
	手 丿 二 兰 手	怕 丨 忄 忄 忄 忄 怕 怕 怕
形	一 二 于 开 形 形 形 形	欸 矢 厶 厶 午 午 年 矢
完	丶 丷 宀 宀 宇 完	欠 丿 亻 ケ 欠
全	丿 人 仝 仝 全 全	认 丶 讠 认 认
瘦	疒 丶 亠 广 广 疒	识 丶 讠 识 识 识
	叟 丿 亻 伫 仃 仃 臼 叟	亲 丶 亠 六 立 立 辛 亲
精	米 丶 丷 半 米 米	身 丿 亻 勺 勾 月 身 身
	青 一 二 韦 韦 青 青 青	体 亻 仁 休 休 休 体

52

VOCABULARY

以前　yǐqián (TW) before, previously

胖　pàng (SV) fat (of a person)

大家　dàjiā (N) everyone

胖子　pàngzi (N) fat person

了　le (P) modal particle indicating change of state

觉得　juéde (V) to feel, sense

每　měi (SP) each, every

睡觉　shuì-jiào (V-O) sleep

别(的)　bié(de) (SP) other, alternative

后来　hòulái (MA) afterwards, later on (refers to past events)

教　jiāo (V) teach

　　教书　jiāo-shū (V-O) teach

打　dǎ (V) hit; fight; play (cards and some ball games)

太极拳　tàijíquán (N) a form of exercise remotely resembling shadow-boxing

情形　qíngxing (N) situation, state of affairs

完全　wánquán (SV/A) complete; completely

一样　yíyàng (SV/A) the same; equally

瘦　shòu (SV) thin, slim

精神　jīngshen (N) spirit, vitality
　　　　(SV) spruce, smart, lively

工作　gōngzuò (N) work
　　　　(V) to work

顿　dùn (M) meal; bout; spell

碗　wǎn (N/M) bowl; bowl of

饿　è (SV) be hungry

饱　bǎo (SV) be full, replete

虽然　suīrán (MA) although

本来　běnlái (MA) originally, in the first place

敢　gǎn (MV) dare to

公斤　gōngjīn (M) kilo (gōng, prefix for metric units)

再　zài (A) again; further, progressively

恐怕　kǒngpà (MA) I'm afraid; perhaps

欸　ê, ēi, āi (I) hey! oi!

认识　rènshi (V) recognize; know

那　nà (MA) then, in that case (= 那么)

父亲　fùqin (N) father

做事　zuò-shì (V-O) work (not limited to occupation)

母亲　mǔqin (N) mother

身体　shēntǐ (N) body; health

怕　pà (V) fear, dread; be afraid of

　　老孙的朋友小王以前很胖,大家都叫他胖子.很多人只知道他叫胖子,不知道他姓什么、叫什么.小王因为太胖了,总是觉得累.每天只想吃饭睡觉,不想做别的事.后来有位朋友教他打太极拳,情形就完全不一样了:人也瘦了,精神也好了.以前不喜欢工作,现在他一个人做两个人的事;以前每顿吃五碗饭还觉得饿,现在两碗就饱了.老孙虽然人不胖,也常常觉得精神不好.他本来很想学学太极拳,可是现在不敢了.小王问他为什么,他说:"你本来很胖,打打太极拳就瘦了,当然很好.我现在只有四十多公斤,要是再瘦,恐怕我这个人就没有了!"

DIALOGUE

王：　欸,老孙,你不认识我了?我是小王啊!

孙：　什么?!胖子小王?你怎么....

王：　瘦了,是不是?

孙：　是啊,你以前不是很胖吗?

王：　以前是很胖,有八十五公斤,现在天天打太极拳,只有六十公斤了.人瘦了,精神也好了.

孙：　我人虽然很瘦,可是常常觉得累,没精神.

王：　你也可以打打太极拳啊!

孙：　我本来很想学学,可是现在不敢了.

王：　为什么?

孙：　你本来很胖,打打太极拳就瘦了,当然很好.我现在只有四十多公斤,要是再瘦,恐怕我这个人就没有了!

(1)

A： 早啊！

B： 早！天气冷了。

A： 是啊，买东西的人也少了。

B： 买东西的人少了，不是因为天气冷吧？

A： 那是因为什么？

B： 恐怕是因为东西贵了。

A： 东西是贵了。去年苹果三毛二一斤，现在五毛四了。

B： 昨天鱼卖八毛五一斤，今天卖一块了。

A： 东西贵了，可是我们的钱还是一样。

B： 所以现在每顿我只能吃一碗饭了！

(2)

A： 怎么样，你们都好吗？

B： 都好，你们呢？

A： 我们也都好，你父亲还做事吗？

B： 他现在太老了，不能工作了。

A： 是不是还爱喝两杯？

B： 酒这么贵，他也不常喝了。

A： 烟还抽吗？

B： 我妈不准他抽，他也不敢抽了。

A： 你母亲身体还那么好吧？

B： 她现在怕胖，不敢吃东西，所以身体不那么好了。

A： 你妹妹还教书吗？

B： 她不教了。她说教书这种工作太累了。

SPEECH PATTERNS

(1) Sentences with modal particle 'le' indicating change of state

(a) Pattern: SV <u>le</u>

他以前很瘦,现在怎么这么胖了?

1. 中文很难吗?   我现在觉得不太难了.
2. 王家有几个孩子?   两个,都大了.
3. 苹果坏了吗?   他买的十公斤苹果都坏了!
4. 会说普通话的人多不多?   以前很少,现在多了.
5. 买个小收音机得多少钱?   现在便宜了,二十五块就够了.
6. 现在你还饿吗?   不饿了。

(b) Pattern: (neg) V (O) <u>le</u>

他怎么不学中文了 ?

1. 再吃一块鱼吧!   不了,谢谢您,我不吃了.
2. 他不怕他父亲吗?   以前很怕,现在不太怕了.
3. 您还有别的事吗?   没有了.
4. 你的好朋友老张怎么样?   老张?! 他不是我的朋友了.
5. 他们有八个孩子,还要生吗?   他们说不生了,谁知道!
6. 你们吃饭吧,不要说话了!   好,不说了.

(c) Pattern: MV V   (O) <u>le</u>

他不敢学 太极拳了.

1. 你会打太极拳吗?   以前会,现在不会了.
2. 他喜欢听音乐吗?   以前不太喜欢,现在很喜欢了.
3. 他们家的孩子都爱看电视吗?   现在大了,不那么爱看了.
4. 电视这么贵,你不想买了吧?
    不想买了,有个收音机就行了.
5. 你们都会说中国话了吧?
    都会说一点儿了,可是还不认识中国字.
6. 你怎么不喝了!   晚上得教书,不能再喝了.

(d) The three above patterns illustrated by means of contrast

1a. 青菜便宜,鸡跟鱼都很贵。
 b. 天气热了,青菜便宜了.

2a. 他们只卖书,不卖地图.
 b. 买地图的人少了,他们不卖地图了.

3a. 他是老李的朋友,我不认识他.
 b. 小王现在这么胖,我完全不认识他了.

4a. 她想学新闻,不想学音乐.
 b. { 她本来想学音乐,现在不想学了.
     她本来学音乐,现在不想学了.

5a. 她爱人没有工作,他们没有钱.
 b. 他们以前很有钱,可是天天吃好的、喝好的,后来就没有钱了.

6a. 他父亲是胖子,他不是胖子.
 b. 他现在只有四十公斤了,不是胖子了.

(2) Modal particle 'le' used to show 'excessiveness'

1. 小张(有)八十五公斤,太胖了.
2. 这种收音机太普通了,家家都有.
3. 他做的那种工作太容易了,我也会做.
4. 对不起,我太累了,我想睡觉了.
5. 他太爱看电视了,没有一天晚上不看.
6. 我太想吃鱼了,今天能不能买一条?
7. 他一个人做十个人的事,精神太好了.
8. 谢谢您,我太饱了,不能再吃了!

(3) <u>Sentences with adverbs used as correlative conjunctions</u>

(a) 只 .... 不/没 ....

    1. 他只会说,不会做。
    2. 这个地方只有咖啡,没有茶。
    3. 他们只卖鱼,不卖别的。
    4. 只准他打人,不准人打他。

(b) 也 .... 也 ....

    1. 大家都想学英文,我们也想学,他们也想学。
    2. 他喜欢吃外国菜,法国菜也吃,德国菜也吃。
    3. 天气好,我们也工作;天气不好,我们也工作。
    4. 这个地方只有这种水果;你吃也可以,不吃也可以。

(c) 虽然 .... 可是 ....

    1. 虽然他父母亲都是中国人,可是他不会说中国话。
    2. 东西虽然很贵,可是还有很多人买。
    3. 工作虽然很忙,可是大家的精神都很好。
    4. 我虽然每天看报,可是不看这种新闻。

(d) 要是 .... 就 ....

    1. 要是他肯说说那天的情形,那就太好了。
    2. 要是你不准我看电视,我就不准你听收音机。
    3. 这么做恐怕不行吧?　要是他说行就行。
    4. 要是你没零钱,就给我一张十块的吧。

(e) 因为 .... 所以 ....

    1. 因为他有很多中国朋友,所以想学点儿中文。
    2. 因为她太爱听音乐了,所以没时间念书。
    3. 他因为身体不好,所以很怕晚上工作。
    4. 他卖的水果都是坏的,所以没人买。

南	nán (L) south	左	zuǒ (L) left, to/on the left
山	shān (N) mountain, hill	右	yòu (L) right, to/on the right
社	shè (N) organized body, society; agency 公社 commune	边	biān [邊] (N) side; border; edge (L-suffix) side
象	xiàng * appearance; image; phenom- enon (N) elephant	竹	zhú * bamboo 竹子
站	zhàn (V) to stand (N) station; (bus) stop	风	fēng [風] (N) wind
最	zuì (A) most, exceedingly (used to form superlative)	景	jǐng * scene, scenery, view
里	lǐ [裏] (L) in, inside	近	jìn (SV) near, close; intimate
员	yuán [員] (N/M) member of group, trade, profession 社员 commune member	写	xiě [寫] (V) to write; to compose
房	fáng * house 房子 ; room (as in 客房 guest room, 书房 study)	信	xìn (V) to believe; to believe in (N) letter; message
头	tóu [頭] (N) head (L-suffix) top; end (SP) first	城	chéng (N) city wall; city
湖	hú (N) lake	玩	wán (V) to play; to have fun, to amuse oneself
树	shù [樹] (N) tree (M:棵 kē) * to set up	决	jué [決] * to decide, to determine (A) definitely (not)

第	**dì** (prefix) ordinal prefix 第一 first;　第二 second	下	**xià** (L) below; down; under; 　　underneath　(SP) next (V) to descend; to alight
次	**cì** (M) time; occasion * inferior, second-rate	广	**guǎng**　　　[廣] (SV) broad; wide; vast 广东 Guangdong (Kwangtung)
路	**lù** (N) road, path; way, route	部	**bù** (N) part, section; govt.dept. (L-suffix) part, section (M) for films, machines, etc.
走	**zǒu** (V) to go, to leave; to walk	桌	**zhuō**　　　* table 桌子　　　　(M:张)
理	**lǐ** (N) reason; principle; logic (V) to put in order	椅	**yǐ**　　　* chair 椅子　　　(M:把 bǎ/张)
快	**kuài** (SV) quick, fast; sharp (of 　　knives) (A) quickly, very soon	底	**dǐ** (N) bottom
到	**dào** (V) to arrive; to reach (CV) to; up until	旁	**páng**　　　* side; other; lateral radical of a Chinese character
向	**xiàng**　　　* towards; to be partial to; direction		

STROKE-ORDER

南	一 十 十 冇 冇 苉 南 南 南	里	丶 口 曰 日 旦 甲 里
山	丨 山 山	员	口 尸 呂 员 员
社	丶 ニ ネ ネ ネ 社 社	房	丶 宀 宀 户 户 户 房 房
象	甴 丿 夕 夕 夕 夕 夕	头	丶 ニ 三 头 头
	豕 丿 门 乛 豸 豸 豕	湖	氵 氵 汁 沽 沽 湖 湖 湖
站	丶 ニ 立 立 立 立 站 站	树	一 十 才 木 杧 枂 树 树
最	日 旦 早 昌 昌 昌 昌 最 最	左	一 ナ ナ 左 左

右　一ナ右
边　フ力力边边
竹　ノ｝ヶ゚ケケ竹竹
风　ノ几凤风
景　日旦昌景
近　ノ゚ケ斤斤沂近
写　丶宀宀写写
信　亻亻广信信
城　一十土圠圹坧城城城
玩　一二干王王玒玒玩
决　丶冫汀江决决
第　竹ノケケケケ竹竹竹
　　弔フコ弓弔弔
次　冫冫冫次次

路　口甲甲跎距趵趵跁路
走　一十土牛未走走
理　二干王玎珥珇珇理理
快　丨丨忄忄忙快快
到　一厶厸至至至到到
何　ノ亻亻冂何
下　一丁下
广　丶亠广
部　亠亠立咅咅部部
桌　丨卜白点卓卓桌
椅　十才木扩梌梌梌梌椅
底　丶亠广广庐庀底底
旁　亠亠立产产旁

VOCABULARY

南 nán (L) south

山 shān (N) mountain, hill

公社 gōngshè (N) commune

气象 qìxiàng (N) meteorology,
　　　weather

站 zhàn (N) station; (bus) stop
　　　(V) to stand

最 zuì (A) most; exceedingly (used
　　　to form superlative)

在 zài (V/CV) to be located in/at

里 lǐ (L) in

员 yuán (N) member of group, trade,
　　　profession

气象员 qìxiàngyuán (N) weatherman

所(儿) suǒ(r) (M) classifier for
　　　houses and some
　　　buildings

房子 fángzi (N) house

头 tóu (N/L-suffix) head; top

前头 qiántou (L/PW) in front

湖 hú (N) lake

后头 hòutou (L/PW) behind

树 shù (N) tree

左 zuǒ (L) left, to/on the left

右 yòu (L) right, to/on the right

边(儿) biān(r) (N/L-suffix) side

竹子 zhúzi (N) bamboo

风景 fēngjǐng (N) scenery

美 měi (SV) beautiful

近 jìn (SV) near, close

    最近 zuìjìn (TW) (just) recently

写 xiě (V) write

信 xìn (N) letter

城 chéng (N) city wall; city

    城里 chéng-li (PW) in town; urban

去 qù (V) to go, go to

玩(儿) wán(r) (V) to play; to amuse oneself

决定 juédìng (V) decide (N) decision

第 dì-(prefix) ordinal prefix

    第一 dìyī (prefix + NU) first

次 cì (M) time; occasion

路 lù (N) road, path; way, route

走 zǒu (V) to go, to leave; to walk

    走路 zǒu-lù (V-O) to walk

地理 dìlǐ (N) geography

快 kuài (SV) quick, fast (A) quickly; very soon

到 dào (V) to arrive, reach (CV) to

上 shàng (L) top; on top of; above

北 běi (L) north

    北边(儿) běibian(r) (L/PW) north

哪边(儿) něibian(r) (QW) where? (which side?)

方向 fāngxiàng (N) direction

那边(儿) nèibian(r) (L/PW) there (that side)

小孩(儿) xiǎohái(r) (N) child

哪儿 nǎr (PW) where? (= nǎlǐ?)

下 xià (L) below; down; under; underneath

西 xī (L) west

东 dōng (L) east

地名 dìmíng (N) place name

部 bù (N/L-suffix) part, section

    南部 nánbù (PW) southern part, the south

那儿 nàr, nèr (L/PW) there (= nàlǐ)

这儿 zhèr (L/PW) here (= zhèlǐ)

桌子 zhuōzi (N) table

椅子 yǐzi (N) chair

底下 dǐxia (L/PW) under; below; beneath

中间 zhōngjiān
中间儿 zhōngjiànr } (L/PW) between; among; in the middle

旁边(儿) pángbiān(r) (L/PW) (by) the side of

女的 nǚ-de (N) female

外 wài (L) outside

南山人民公社一共有五个气象站.最小的那个在大山里.
只有一个气象员叫小张,是我的老同学.这个气象站虽然只是
一所儿普通的房子,可是前头有湖,后头有树,左右两边儿都是
竹子,风景很美.小张很喜欢这个地方,可是他一个人在山里,没
有朋友.最近写信给我跟小王,请我们这两个城里人去玩儿.昨
天天气很好,我跟小王决定去看看他.我们两个人都是第一次
去.大家都说山里的路不好找,本来应该先问问别人怎么走.小
王说他有地图,看地图就行了.他是学地理的,我当然得听他的,
可是.....

DIALOGUE

A: 小王,我太饿了,不能再走了!

B: 快到了,快到了.欸!地图上怎么没有这所儿房子啊?

A: 气象站应该在北边儿,可是哪边儿是北啊?

B: 我现在也不知道方向了.欸!你看,那边儿有个小孩儿,我们去问问他.

A: 小朋友,这是什么地方?

C: 这是我家.

B: 这山里是不是有个气象站?

C: 我们老师说有.

A: 你知道在哪儿吗?

C: 我们老师说就在湖边儿.

B: 哪个湖边儿?那个湖在什么地方呢?

C: 我们老师说那个湖叫小明湖,在北边儿.

A: 那么,你知道哪边儿是北吗?

C: 你看你的地图吧,我们老师说,上北下南,左西右东,地图的上
   边儿就是北!

(1)

A：我想问你两个中国地名好不好？

B：我知道一点儿中国地理，你问吧！

A：山东在哪儿？

B：山东在山西的东边儿。

A：湖南呢？

B：湖南在湖北的南边儿。

A：广西呢？

B：广西在广东的西边儿。

A：可是广东在哪儿呢？

B：广东当然在广西的东边儿。

A：这我也知道。我要问的是广东在中国什么地方？

B：不是在中国的南部吗？

(2)

A：今天的报在你那儿吗？

B：不在我这儿，是不是在你后头的桌子上？

A：没有啊！噢！在这儿，在椅子底下。

B：我今天还没时间看报，有什么新闻？

A：报上说东西都贵了。

B：那不是新闻！

A：最近找工作很难了。

B：那也不是新闻！欸！快、快，你看！电视上这三个人，中间那个是不是小李？

A：是小李，他旁边儿那个女的是谁？

B：不认识，我不知道他有一位这么好看的女朋友。

(1) Directions and place words

(a) Compass directions

东	E		东 南	SE	
南	S		东 北	NE	
西	W		西 南	SW	
北	N		西 北	NW	

(b) Relative place words

上 头 / 上 边	东 边 儿
下 头 / 下 边	南 边 儿
里 头 / 里 边	西 边 儿
外 头 / 外 边	北 边 儿
前 头 / 前 边	东 南 边 儿
后 头 / 后 边	西 北 边 儿
左 边	北 部
右 边	东 南 部
中 间 / 中 间 儿	这 边 ～ 这 里 = 这 儿
底 下	那 边 ～ 那 里 = 那 儿
	哪 边?～ 哪 里?= 哪 儿?

(c) Place-word phrases

房 子 (的) 前 头 / 前 边	气 象 站 (的) 北 边
大 山 (的) 后 头 / 后 边	英 国 (的) 南 边
城 外 头 / 外 边; 城 外	中 国 (的) 西 北 部
湖 里 头 / 里 边; 湖 里	我 这 儿
树 (的) 上 头 / 上 边; 树 上	你 那 儿
山 (的) 下 头 / 下 边; 山 下	老 王 那 儿
你 (的) 左 边	书 上
地 图 (的) 右 边	信 上
树 (的) 底 下	报 上
路 (的) 中 间 / 中 间 儿	字 典 里

(2) 'Zài' as main verb with complement

Pattern:　　N　　_zài_　　PW

报　在　哪儿？　在桌子上.

1. 你家在哪儿？　　我家在城外头.
2. 有人在家吗？　　哪位？
3. 你说的那所儿房子在哪儿？　　就在东湖南边儿.
4. 他工作的地方在城里头吗？　　不在城里头,在山上.
5. 她给我的信在哪儿？　　就在桌子上,字典旁边儿.
6. 你的钱呢？　　都在我爱人那儿！
7. 方向对吗？　　对,你看西湖不是在我们左边儿吗？

(3) Existence in a place

Pattern:　　PW　　_yǒu_　　N

中国　有　很多大山.

1. 英国北部有没有大湖？　　有,有不少风景很美的大湖.
2. 山上有很多房子,每所儿房子前头都有苹果树.
3. 桌子上有杯茶,不知道是谁的.
4. 东湖西边儿有一条大路,路的两边儿都是竹子.
5. 城里有个卖鱼的地方,那儿的鱼很便宜.
6. 我这儿没有他要的那个东西.

　　Contrast:　我没有他要的那个东西.

(4) Collocations including PW suffixes

1. 报上没有这个新闻.
2. 书上说这种竹子只有中国有.
3. 字典里没有这个字吗？　　没有.
4. 他信上说最近工作很忙,可是身体很好.
5. 我这张地图上有两个西山.
6. 收音机上说最近买房子的人少了.

(5) Modification by place expressions

1. 房子后头的树都是苹果树吗?
2. 老张旁边儿的那个女的是谁?　　那是他妹妹.
3. 我很喜欢湖中间儿的那所儿小房子.
4. 椅子上的那本地理书是谁的?
5. 他最想吃的就是西湖里的鱼.
6. 你每天晚上都看电视上的新闻吗?

(6) The particle 'le' indicating imminent action

1. 北京快到了吗?　　快了!快了!
2. 我要睡觉了,不能再吃了.
3. 他几岁?　　快八岁了.
4. 难不难?　　不太难,我快会了.
5. 他的生日就要到了,你决定送他什么?
6. 新闻时间快到了,我们听听新闻吧!
7. 天气快要冷了,我得去买毛衣了.

(7) Stative verbs as adverbs

1. 他家在城里头,很容易找.
2. 中文很难学吗?　　不难学!
3. 中国菜好吃,可是不好做.(=难做)
4. 这件事很难决定吗?　　很难决定,我们问问别的人吧.
5. 湖边儿的风景真好看.
6. 这个音乐很好听.
7. 他送我的那瓶酒不好喝.
8. 老王请客,人多菜少,不够吃.
9. 我想写信问问他北京有什么好玩儿的地方.

傅	fù * tutor, teacher 师傅 master worker, skilled craftsman	店	diàn (N) shop, store; inn
铁	tiě [鐵] (N) iron	售	shòu * (LC) to sell, to retail
厂	chǎng [廠] (N) factory, mill, plant	弟	dì * younger brother 弟弟
男	nán * man, male (of persons)	农	nóng * [農] agriculture, farming 农民 peasant
已	yǐ (A) already (LC) to cease	搞	gǎo (V) to do; to make; to go in for; to set up; to get hold of
经	jīng * [經] to pass through; to undergo; a sacred book, classic	利	lì (N) advantage; profit, interest * favourable; to benefit
解	jiě [解] (V) to undo; to liberate * to explain; to solve	干	gàn [幹] (V) to do, to work * trunk; main part 干部 cadre
放	fàng (V) to let go; to let out/off; to place	错	cuò [錯] (SV) wrong, mistaken (N) fault, error 不错 that's right; not bad
军	jūn [軍] army, armed forces; military 军人 serviceman	化	huà (V) to change, transform; to melt * -ize, -ify
百	bǎi (NU) hundred	平	píng (SV) flat, level, even, smooth
货	huò [貨] (N) goods, commodity	高	gāo (SV) high; tall a surname
商	shāng * trade, commerce, business; to discuss, to consult the Shang dynasty	哥	gē * elder brother 哥哥

着	zháo [着] (V) to touch * to catch; to suffer; to be troubled with	单	dān * [單] single; odd; singly; only; alone; list (as in 名单 name list, 菜单 menu)
急	jí (SV) hurried; worried; impatient; irritated; urgent	象	xiàng [像]+ (V) to resemble (SV) similar, alike (N) portrait; statue
语	yǔ * [語] speech; language; dialect 汉语 the Chinese language	产	chǎn * [產] to produce, to yield; product; property; real estate
替	tì (V) to substitute for; to take the place of (CV) for; on behalf of	队	duì [隊] (N) team; group (M) for groups of men, warships, aeroplanes, etc.
星	xīng (N) star	介	jiè * be situated between
期	qī * a period of time; scheduled time 星期 week (M) an issue	绍	shào * [紹] to continue; to connect
办	bàn [辦] (V) to do, handle, manage; to see to; to punish (by law)	安	ān * * peaceful; quiet; safe (V) to install; to fix on
久	jiǔ (SV) long protracted (time)	局	jú * bureau, office; situation (M) for games, sets, innings (of chess, tennis, etc.)

+ full-form still in use in situations where ambiguity may arise

STROKE–ORDER

傅	亻	解	角 ⁿ 𠂤 𦥑 角
	甫 一 厂 万 甫 甫 甫 甫		罕 ㄱ ㄲ ㄲ ㄲ ㄲ 罕
	寸 一 寸 寸	放	亠 亠 方 方 㚣 㚣 放
铁	丿 丿 𠂉 𠂢 钅 钅 钅 铁 铁 铁	军	冖 冖 𠃊 𠌂 军
厂	一 厂	百	一 丆 丆 百 百 百
男	丶 口 曰 田 田 畀 男	货	亻 亻 化 化 𧴲 货 货
已	ㄱ ㄱ 已	商	亠 六 产 产 商 商
经	乚 纟 纟 纟 纟 经	店	亠 广 广 庐 店

售　亻 亻 信 佳 佳 售
弟　丷 丷 当 兰 弟 弟
农　一 少 农 农 农
搞　扌 扩 拮 搞 搞
利　丿 二 千 禾 禾 利 利
干　一 二 干
错　钅 丿 ナ 钅 钅
昔　一 ナ 卄 芯 昔
化　亻 亻 化
平　一 ㇆ 刁 立 平
高　亠 古 高 高
哥　一 可 可 哥 哥
着　羊 丷 丷 兰 羊
目　丨 冂 月 目
急　丿 勹 刍 刍 急

语　丶 讠 订 订 诏 语
替　二 丰 夫 扗 玣 鈇 替
星　日 旦 旦 星 星
期　其 一 ㇀ 卄 甘 其 其
月　丿 刀 月
办　丁 力 办 办
久　丿 勹 久
单　丷 丷 㑇 㓂 白 旦 单
象 (像)　𠂉 ㄅ 多 争 象 象 象
产　亠 六 立 产
队　阝 阝 队 队
介　丿 人 介 介
绍　ㄥ 纟 纟 纫 绍
安　丶 宀 宀 安 安
局　一 ㇆ 尸 局 局

VOCABULARY

师傅 shīfu (N) master craftsman; old hand

铁 tiě (N) iron

(工)厂 (gōng)chǎng (N) factory, works, mill

工人 gōngrén (N) worker, workman

小学 xiǎoxué (N) junior school

男 nán (AT) male

已经 yǐjing (A) already

解放军 jiěfàngjūn (N) Liberation Army; member of same

　解放 jiěfàng (V) liberate (N) liberation

百货商店 bǎihuò shāngdiàn (N) 'hundred goods shop', i.e. (department) store

(商)店 (shāng)diàn (N) shop, store

当 dāng (CLV) be (in position of), serve as

售货员 shòuhuòyuán (N) 'sell goods person'— shop assistant

姐妹 jiěmèi (N) sisters (older and younger)

弟弟 dìdi (N) younger brother

大学 dàxué (N) university

农 nóng (N) agriculture

搞 gǎo (V) do, go in for, make, get up to

70

水利　shuǐlì (N) water conservancy

干部　gànbù (N) cadre

错　cuò (N) mistake
　　　(SV) wrong, in error

　不错　bú-cuò (IE) that's right;
　　　not bad, pretty good

文化　wénhuà (N) culture; (standard
　　　of) education

水平　shuǐpíng (N) level, standard

高　gāo (SV) high; tall

对象　duìxiàng (N) object (of affec-
　　　tion); girlfriend or
　　　boyfriend

做　zuò (CLV) be, act as, serve as

哥哥　gēge (N) elder brother

为　wèi (CV) because of, for the sake
　　　of

着急　zháojí (V) worry about
　　　(SV) anxious, worried

外语　wàiyǔ (N) foreign language

替　tì (CV) on behalf of, for
　　　(V) to stand in for

星期日/天　xīngqī-rì/tiān (TW)
　　　Sunday

　星期　xīngqī (N) week

给　gěi (CV) for; in the interests of

办　bàn (V) do, manage, see to

　办事　bàn shì (VO) see to matters,
　　　business

好久不见　hǎo jiǔ bú jiàn (IE)
　　　long time no see

单位　dānwèi (N) unit; place of work

好象　hǎoxiàng (MA) seemingly, as if

生产队　shēngchǎnduì (N) production
　　　team

　生产　shēngchǎn (V) produce
　　　(N) production

大队　dàduì (N) 'big team'— brigade

机会　jīhuì (N) opportunity

介绍　jièshao (V) introduce
　　　(N) introduction

　给人介绍　gěi rén jièshao (PH)
　　　effect an introduction
　　　for somebody

晚　wǎn (SV) late

(是)真的　(shì) zhēn de (SV) be true

书店　shūdiàn (N) bookshop

人民日报　Rénmín Rìbào (PR) People's
　　　Daily

公安局　gōng'ānjú (N) public security
　　　bureau

别　bié (=不要) don't (negative
　　　imperative)

叫　jiào (V) tell; order

中学　zhōngxué (N) middle school

问 X 好　wèn X hǎo (IE) ask after, give
　　　regards to X

李师傅是我们城里一个铁工厂的老工人,他爱人在第八小学教书.他们有两个孩子,一男一女,都已经二十多了.男孩子是解放军,不常在家;女孩子在百货商店当售货员.老李没有姐妹,只有一个弟弟叫李明道,以前在大学学农,现在在青山人民公社搞水利,是个干部,人很不错,文化水平也高,可是今年已经三十五了,还没有对象.因为父母亲都不在了,这个做哥哥的常常为这件事着急.最近弟弟想学外语,写信请哥哥替他在城里买两本书.今天星期日,老李就去给弟弟办这件事,在路上......

DIALOGUE

王: 欸!李师傅,好久不见,还认识我吗?

李: 小王!当然认识,好久不见!现在在哪个单位工作啊?

王: 三〇六厂,还是当工人.

李: 那好啊,有几个孩子了?

王: 两个,一男一女,不能再生了.

李: 欸,小王,你好象有个妹妹,是不是?

王: 是啊,现在在青山公社.

李: 青山公社?!我弟弟也在青山啊,你妹妹在哪个生产队?

王: 好象是东湖大队.

李: 太好了!我弟弟也在东湖,有机会能不能给他们介绍介绍,我弟弟还没......

王: 太晚了!我妹妹已经有对象了.

李: 噢?!真的?!

王: 当然是真的,她对象也姓李,就在他们社里搞水利,好象叫李明道.

李: 什么?!李明道!那不就是我弟弟吗!

(1)

A：好久不见,家里人都好吧?

B：都好.最近还是那么忙吗?

A：一样.欸,你哥哥现在在哪个单位工作啊?

B：在二中教书.

A：你姐姐呢?

B：在新华书店当售货员.

A：你弟弟还在二〇四厂吗?

B：不,他不在工厂了.现在是我们社里的气象员,在山上工作.

A：你妹妹不在人民日报了吧?

B：还在.她就喜欢搞新闻工作.

A：你知道我现在在哪个单位吗?

B：不知道.噢!我知道了,是不是在公安局?

(2)

A：不早了,我得走了!

B：别走了,就在我们这儿吃饭吧!

A：不了,谢谢.我还得去给我妹妹买东西.

B：他们还在山上吗?

A：是啊.她说山上已经冷了,叫我替她买件毛衣.

B：他们有几个孩子了?

A：三个了,都还小.天天为这三个孩子忙.

B：她爱人呢?

A：她爱人最近替朋友在城里的中学教书,很少在家.

B：现在大家好象都很忙,你要是写信,请你替我问他们好!

(1) Verbal expressions in series

(a) First verb as functive verb
(the verbs in series are marked by dots)

1. 明天是我们家老二的生日, 我们想买个东西给他。
2. (他)写信给我跟小王, 请我们这两个城里人去玩儿。
3. 晚上有客人, 我得去买菜。
4. 他想做顿法国菜吃。
5. 你为什么不买瓶好酒喝?
6. 山里没人, 他很想找个朋友说话。
7. 他父母要送他去学农, 可是他想学音乐。
8. 他那儿没有书店, 他写信请他哥哥替他买书。
9. 第五中学要找人教外语, 你可以介绍我去吗?
10. 你们有饭吃, 有书念, 还要什么?

(b) First verb as coverb
(the coverbs are marked by dots)

1. 对不起, 这儿不准说上海话, 请你用普通话说。
2. 星期三我不能去, 请你替我跟老师说一说。
3. 他给的钱太少了, 没人肯给他做事。
4. 谁给这三个孩子做饭?
5. 你想跟谁学中文?
6. 我不爱跟那种人说话。
7. 你怎么能用你父母给你买书的钱买酒喝呢?   我知道我错了。
8. 请你替我用中国话跟他们说一说, 好不好?
9. 你三十五了, 还没对象, 我真为你着急!
10. 别着急了, 给我介绍一位女朋友就行了。
11. 不准给他写信: a. 不准写信给他。
                 b. 不准替他写信。

(2) 'Zài' as coverb giving setting for main action

Pattern:　　S　zài　PW　V　(O)
他　在　小学　教书.

1. 今天晚上没事,我想在家看看书、写写信.
2. 张家的老二、老三都在二中念书吗?　　不错,都在二中.
3. 你喜欢在外国工作吗?　　这很难说.
4. 天气太热了,很多人在房子外头睡觉.
5. 他想在城外搞个小工厂.
6. 孩子们好象都爱在海边玩儿.
7. 她不在那个商店买东西,她说那儿的东西贵.
8. 在城里找工作很不容易,机会太少了.
9. 他说那个地方就在上海的西南边儿,请你在地图上找找.
10a. 他不在家喝酒. (他在哪儿喝酒?在家喝吗?)
  b. 他在家不喝酒. (他在家喝不喝酒?)

(3) Modification of nouns by clauses containing place expressions

Pattern:　　zài　PW　V　O　de　N
在　商店　买东西　的　人

1. 那天在你家吃饭的那位先生是不是学农的?
2. 在这个大学教书的老师都是英国人吗?
3. 没有人认识那位在那儿喝酒的老太太.
4. 在树上吃苹果的那两个孩子是谁家的?
5. 在东湖前边卖报的那个人以前是学新闻的.
6. 我很想知道那位天天在大学前边打太极拳的老先生多少岁了.
7. 那位就是在我们公社搞水利的李师傅,以前是解放军.
8. 我那位在公安局工作的朋友,外语水平很高,也很会办事.

(4) <u>Classificatory verbs relating to job, status, function, etc.</u>

1. 他两个弟弟都在第一铁工厂当工人.
2. 很多人都想当百货商店的售货员.
3. 在这儿当老师的都喜欢喝酒吗?
4. 小王想当解放军,可是不够高.
5. 做父母的谁不爱儿女?
6. 老王说话很不好听,没人喜欢跟他做朋友.
7. 做客人的当然不能说菜不好吃.

(5) <u>Subject-predicate predicates</u>

1. 他哥哥人好象不错.
2. 他弟弟身体不错,人也精神.
3. 我妹妹念书好,办事不行.
4. 老张人高,文化也高.
5. 中国地大人多.
6. 这地方前头有湖,后头有山,风景真不错.
7. 他爱人做的菜,鸡好吃,鱼不好吃.
8. 今天星期天,每个商店人都很多.
9. 山上树多,房子少.
10a. 他妹妹工作好.
  b. 他妹妹的工作好.

伦	lún * [倫] human relationships	谈	tán [談] (V) to talk, chat, discuss, negotiate 谈天儿 to chat
敦	dūn * honest, sincere 伦敦 London	题	tí [題] * topic, subject, title (V) to inscribe
馆	guǎn [館] (N) house; establishment; hall; shop (of service trades), as 饭馆 restaurant	旅	lǚ * travel (M) an army brigade 旅行 travel, tour
从	cóng [從] (CV) from (LC) to follow	活	huó (V) to live (SV) alive, living; lively (N) work; workmanship
兴	xìng * [興] mood or desire to do sth; interest; excitement	直	zhí (SV) straight, straight- forward; vertical (A) continuously
趣	qù * interest; delight	等	děng (V) to wait (for) (M) grade, class * and so on, etc.
影	yǐng * shadow; reflection; image 电影 film, movie	火	huǒ (N) fire; anger (SV) angry (AT) fiery
更	gèng (A) more, still more, still...-er, further	车	chē [車] (N) vehicle (M: 辆 liàng) * machine
开	kāi [開] (V) to open (up/out); to start; to operate (machines, vehicles), run (a business)	过	guò [過] (V) to pass (through), to cross; to spend (time) a verb suffix
始	shǐ * beginning, start 开始 (V/N) start	苏	sū * [蘇] (LC) to revive short for Suzhou, Jiangsu, Soviet and USSR
习	xí * [習] to practise; to get accus- tomed to; habit, custom	联	lián * [聯] to unite, to ally oneself with 苏联 Soviet Union
千	qiān (NU) thousand	舒	shū * to unfold; to relax; leisurely

服	fú * clothes, dress (V) to yield to	清	qīng (SV) clear, pure the Qing (Ch'ing) dynasty
长	cháng　　　[長] (SV) long	楚	chǔ　　　* clear, neat
算	suàn (V) to calculate, reckon, 　　compute; to regard as	必	bì　　　* must, have to; necessary 必得 must;　不必 need not
带	dài　　　[帶] (V) to bring, to take along; 　　to lead (N) belt, band, zone	历	lì　　　*　[歷] to pass through, to undergo; to experience
汽	qì (N) vapour, steam 汽车 motor car	史	shǐ (N) history a surname
票	piào (N) ticket; coupon　(M: 张)	便	biàn　　　* convenient, handy; informal; to relieve oneself: 小便 uri- nate; 大便 defecate
戏	xì　　　[戲] (N) drama, play, show 京戏 Peking opera	换	huàn　　　[換] (V) to change, exchange
往	wàng (CV) to, towards (LC) to go to	转	zhuǎn　　　[轉] (V) to turn; to pass on; to 　　transfer
飞	fēi　　　[飛] (V) to fly	场	chǎng　　　[場] * a place, a field (M) for performances; spell 　　of
又	yòu (A) again, then again; on 　　top of (that)	停	tíng (V) to stop, halt, pause; 　　to park, berth
些	xiē (NU/M) some, several; amount		

STROKE—ORDER

伦　亻伣伶伦
敦　亠亡亨亨享敦敦敦

馆　饣丿勹饣
官　丶宀宀宀官官

78

从　丿　亻　从　从

兴　丶　丷　兴　兴　兴

趣　走　一　十　土　キ　キ　走　走
　　取　一　丆　冂　月　耳　取　取

影　日　旦　昌　景　景　影

更　一　一　一　一　百　更　更

开　一　二　于　开

始　く　女　女　如　如　始

习　丁　习　习

千　丿　一　千

谈　讠　讠　讠　讠　说　谈　谈　谈

题　日　旦　早　早　昰　是　昆　题　题

旅　一　亠　方　方　扩　旅　旅

活　氵　氵　氵　氵　活

直　一　十　广　古　直　直

等　竹　竹　竺　笋　等　等

火　丶　丷　少　火　丿　丶　少　少　火

车　一　七　左　车

过　一　寸　寸　过　过

苏　一　艹　艻　芀　苏　苏

联　一　丆　月　耳　耳　耶　联　联

舒　人　合　今　舍　舍　舒　舒　舒

服　丿　几　月　月　肝　服　服

长　丿　一　七　长

算　竹　竹　笡　笪　算　算　算

带　一　一　一　卅　卅　带　带

汽　氵　氵　氵　沪　汽

票　一　一　西　西　覀　票

戏　刁　又　圣　戏　戏　戏

往　彳　彳　彳　往　往

飞　乁　飞　飞

又　刁　又

此　丨　ト　止　止　此　此

清　氵　氵　氵　泔　清　清

楚　木　林　棘　梺　梺　梺　楚

必　丶　心　心　必　必

历　一　厂　历　历

史　丶　口　口　史　史

便　亻　亻　伫　佰　佰　便　便

换　扌　扩　护　拘　换　换

转　车　一　七　车　车
　　专　二　专　专

场　丶　十　土　圴　场

停　亻　亻　伫　佰　偟　停

VOCABULARY

伦敦 Lúndūn (PW) London

图书馆 túshūguǎn (N) library

从 cóng (CV) from (used of time and space)

兴趣 xìngqù (N) interest (directed towards, not inherent in something)

　　对 X 有兴趣 take an interest in X

电影(儿) diànyǐng(r) (N) motion picture

更 gèng (A) still more, even more

前 qián (L) before, ago

开始 kāishǐ (V/N) start

　　从……开始 starting from……

学习 xuéxí (V/N) 'learn + practise' — study

千 qiān (NU) thousand

谈天(儿) tán-tiān(r) (V-O) chat, natter

问题 wèntí (N) issue, question, problem

早就 zǎojiù (A) long since

旅行 lǚxíng (V/N) travel

平常 píngcháng (SV/MA) usual, every-day, ordinary; usually

生活 shēnghuó (N/V) life; live

一直 yìzhí (A) straight through, all along, directly

法子 fázi/fǎzi (N) way, means, method

没法子 méi fázi/fǎzi (IE) have no way of; can't be helped

等 děng (V) wait (for) (N/M) grade, class

坐 zuò (V) sit (on) (CV) travel by; by

火车 huǒchē (N) train

经过 jīngguò (V) pass through (CV) by, by way of

苏联 Sūlián (PW) Soviet Union

舒服 shūfu (SV) comfortable

不舒服 (SV) uncomfortable (IE) not feel well

长 cháng (SV) long

打算 dǎsuàn (V) reckon on, have in mind to, plan to

带 dài (V) bring, take along

小说 xiǎoshuō (N) (work of) fiction, novel

公共汽车 gōnggòng qìchē (N) 'public motor car'—— bus

票 piào (N) ticket, coupon

戏 xì (N) drama, play, show

往 wàng (CV) in direction of, towards; bound for (also pro-nounced wǎng)

飞机 fēijī (N) aeroplane

又 yòu (A) again, then again

又....又.... both ....and....

(一)些 (yì)xiē (M) some, several, a small amount

国家 guójiā (N) state, country

清楚 qīngchu (SV) clear

干吗 gànmá? (IE) do what? get up to what? what for?

必,必得 bì, bìděi (MV) must, have to

不必 bú bì no need to

历史 lìshǐ (N) history; history book

电车 diànchē (N) tram

方便 fāngbiàn (SV) convenient

换 huàn (V) change, exchange

换车 huàn chē (V O) change trains or buses

车站 chēzhàn (N) station, (bus) stop

过 guò (V) pass, cross

路口(儿) lùkǒu(r) (N/PW) 'road mouth' —— turning, intersection

向 xiàng (CV) toward(s)

转 zhuǎn (V) turn

场 chǎng (M) for performances; spell of

日本 Rìběn (PW) Japan

请客 qǐng-kè (V-O) invite guest; stand treat

开 kāi (V) open (up/out); start; operate

开车 kāi-chē (V-O) drive

停 tíng (V) stop, halt; park, berth

地铁 dìtiě (N) short for dìxià tiědào, 'underground railway', tube

PRESENTATION

老钱在伦敦城里的一个图书馆工作.他从小就对中国有兴趣:爱看中国电影儿,爱听中国音乐,更爱吃中国菜,几年前开始学习中文.现在已经认识两、三千个汉字.跟中国朋友谈天儿,看普通的中文书报,都没有什么大问题.他早就想到中国去旅行,看看中国人平常的生活情形,可是因为他的钱总是不够,所以一直没法子去.最近他觉得不能再等了,就决定坐火车经过苏联去北京.虽然路上得走八九天,一定很累,一定很不舒服,可是这是去中国最便宜的法子.他朋友问他,在火车上的时间那么长,他都打算做什么,是不是得带几十本小说看?他说他不带小说,他不带小说带什么呢?

DIALOGUE

A: 欸,老钱!你在这儿等谁啊?

B: 等谁?!我不等谁!我等公共汽车到城里去买票.

A: 买什么票?是戏票还是电影票?

B: 都不是,我去买火车票.

A: 要去旅行啊?是不是到北边儿去?

B: 不,我往东走,到中国去.

A: 什么?!坐火车到中国去?那得走多少天啊?

B: 不要多少天,八、九天就够了.

A: 从这儿到中国也有飞机啊,为什么不坐飞机呢?又快又舒服.

B: 谁不知道坐飞机又快又舒服,可是我的钱只够买一张二等火车票,没法子!

A: 坐火车都经过哪些国家啊?

B: 我还不太清楚,只知道一定要经过苏联.

A: 这条路真不近,在火车上的时间那么长,你都想干吗?恐怕得带几十本小说吧?

B: 不必,我只带一本中国历史就够了,这条路虽然长,可是中国的历史不是更长吗?

SKETCHES

(1)

A: 到哪儿去啊?

B: 我到西城去。

A: 这么晚了,又这么冷,到西城去干吗?

B: 没法子,我得去看个朋友。

A: 你打算怎么去啊?

B: 我这是第一次去,不知道是坐电车好,还是坐公共汽车好。

A: 你朋友家在西城什么地方?

B: 他说就在西城图书馆后头。

A: 那我知道,坐电车去方便,一○九路一直可以到图书馆,不用换车。

B: 您知道一○九路车站在哪儿吗?

A: 很近,从这儿往北走,过两个路口儿,向右转,百货商店前头就是。

B: 多谢、多谢!

A: 不谢。

(2)

A: 今天星期六,晚上打算到哪儿去玩儿?

B: 不想到哪儿去,你呢?

A: 想去看场日本电影儿,你有没有兴趣啊?

B: 你请客,我就去。

A: 没问题!你请我吃晚饭,我就请你看电影儿。

B: 行!我们去吃顿日本饭怎么样?

A: 好啊,现在就走吧,我开车。

B: 城里车那么多,又没地方停,还是坐地铁去吧!

A: 那太不方便了,中间儿要换车,两头儿还得走路。

B: 你怕走路啊?大家都说走路对身体好。

A: 你的身体已经够好了,不必再走路了,还是坐我的车去吧。

SPEECH PATTERNS

(1) Coming and going

Pattern: 中国人来(英国), 英国人去(中国).

1. 他今天来不来?　　他昨天说一定来.
2. 你们都去吗?　　要是有人开车,我们就都去.
3. 他信上说什么?　　他说他很想来伦敦.
4. 学中文的都应该去中国吗?　　我觉得都应该去.
5. 谁去谁那儿?　　我们这儿地方大,你们来我们这儿吧.
6. 每年来英国的外国人真不少.
   是啊,去外国的英国人也很多.
7. 他想去北京,可是没钱,怎么办?　　没法子.

(2) To and fro

Patterns:　a.　　cóng/dào　X　lái/qù
　　　　　　　我　从/到图书馆来/去.
　　　　　b.　　cóng　X　dào　Y　lái/qù
　　　　　　　他要从　法国　到　德国　去.

1. 早啊,你从哪儿来?　　我从家里来.
2. 你到哪儿去?　　我到老王那儿去.
3. 星期天不工作,没人到这儿来吗?　　平常很少人来.
4. 他们都想到山上去,你怎么不去?　　山也太高,我也太胖.
5. 你们明天到青山公社,从哪儿去啊?　　我们从厂里去.
6. 我早就想到日本去,可是一直没机会.
7. 从湖北到广东(去)一定得经过湖南吗?
8. 从星期一到星期五他每天要学五十个汉字.
9. 从昨天晚上开始,外国人不准再到城外头去了.
10. 从报上可以知道现在英国的问题很多.

(3) Means of conveyance

Pattern: 我每天坐公共汽车来。

1. 你们到中国去,打算怎么去?　　我们坐火车去。
2. 从伦敦到北京,坐飞机(去)得多少钱?
   普通票恐怕得一千多块吧。
3. 老李说你要到法国去,坐火车去吗?　　不,我坐朋友的车去。
4. 从这儿到城外的东湖有电车吗?
   没有电车,我们得坐公共汽车去。
5. 去他们家,坐几路车?　　他们家很近,不必坐车,走路去就行了。
6. 你说我们怎么去好?
   走路去吧,天气这么好,走走不是很舒服吗?
7. 从伦敦坐火车到上海要多少天?路上得停多少站?
8. 从你家坐公共汽车到大学得多少钱?　　六毛五。
9a. 你们怎么去火车站?　　我们坐地铁去。
 b. 去火车站怎么走?
   从这儿一直往东走,过三个路口儿,向左转就是。

(4) Purposes in coming and going

Patterns:　a. 我去吃饭。
　　　　　 b. 我吃饭去。
　　　　　 c. 我去吃饭去。

1. 你最想去什么地方旅行?　　中国。
2. (到)哪儿去?　　去城里看戏去。
3. 他到山上去干吗?　　他去学太极拳。
4. 再喝杯茶吧?　　不了,我还得到火车站去送朋友。
5. 有机会很想到中国去工作。　　你是学什么的。
6. 这些人到我们大学来干吗?　　他们来看图书馆。
7. 他不想在生产队了,想到山上去搞气象去。
8. 没事儿,请常到我们这儿来玩儿!　　好,一定!

(5) Question words as indefinites

1. 您要买什么？　　a. 我想买张桌子。
　　　　　　　　　b. 我不买什么，看看可以吗？

2. 今天晚上到哪儿去？　　a. 我想跟朋友去看电影儿。
　　　　　　　　　　　　b. 不到哪儿去，我想在家看看电视。

3. 他有多少中文书？　　a. 最少有五、六千本。
　　　　　　　　　　　b. 没有多少，最多二、三十本。

4. 那些国家的生活水平怎么样？　　a. 很高。
　　　　　　　　　　　　　　　　b. 不怎么高。

5. 这些问题你都清楚吗？　　a. 很清楚。
　　　　　　　　　　　　　b. 不怎么清楚。

6. 你对历史小说有兴趣吗？　　a. 很有兴趣。
　　　　　　　　　　　　　　b. 不怎么有兴趣。
　　　　　　　　　　　　or 没什么兴趣。

7. 你打算给谁写信？　　a. 我打算给老李写信。
　　　　　　　　　　　b. 我不打算给谁写信。

8. 你什么地方不舒服？　　a. 我的头不太舒服。
　　　　　　　　　　　　b. 我没什么地方不舒服。

9. 西山公社有几个工厂？　　a. 三个。
　　　　　　　　　　　　　b. 没几个。

　　Compare：西山公社有几个工厂，工人一共有三、四百。

10. 你有几个华侨朋友？　　a. 十几个。
　　　　　　　　　　　　b. 没几个。

　　Compare：我有几个华侨朋友，他们只会说广东话。

(6) 'Dōu' used to indicate plurality in a question

1. 你都想吃什么？　　我想吃点儿鸡，也想吃点儿鱼。
2. 你们都对什么有兴趣？
　　他们三个人对地理有兴趣，我们五个人对历史有兴趣。

85

3. 他们都姓什么？　　一个姓李，一个姓钱，还有两个姓王。

4. 明天星期天，你都想干吗？　　我想去买东西，也想去看电影儿。

5. 你带这么多钱，都想买什么啊？
   我得买很多东西：毛衣、字典、收音机.....

6. 他们都去哪些国家？
   他们要去法国、德国、苏联、日本跟中国。

(7) More elaborate choice-type questions

```
Patterns:    a.       O.... O.... ?
                    你 累 不 累 ?
                    这个好，那个好 ?
             b.    shì  A  (ne), shì  B  (ne) ?
                    你是 去 (呢)，是 不去 (呢) ?
                     是中文难(呢)，是英文难(呢) ?
             c.    shì  A  (ne), háishì  B  (ne) ?
                    你是喜欢 (呢)，还是不喜欢 (呢) ?
                     是他去 (呢)，还是 你去 (呢) ?
```

1. 你说茶好喝，咖啡好喝？　　我说咖啡好喝。

2. 是你认识的字多，还是他认识的字多？
   我们两个人认识的字一样多。

3. 是他来还是你去？　　他也不来，我也不去。

4. 今天晚上吃鱼好，还是吃鸡好？　　我说还是吃鱼好。

5. 你们怎么去？坐火车还是坐飞机？
   飞机票太贵，我们坐火车去。

6. 她是喜欢看电影儿呢，还是喜欢看戏？　　好象都不太喜欢。

7. 那个商店(是)在车站东边儿，还是在车站西边儿？
   我也不太清楚。

8. 坐地铁去方便，还是坐公共汽车去方便？
   公共汽车方便：一一三路一直可以到，不必换车。

9. 是在公社搞生产容易，还是在山上搞气象容易？
   都不容易。

10. 是你的汉语水平高，还是她的汉语水平高？　　都不太高。

86

晨	chén * morning	面	miàn * face; surface; side; aspect
钟	zhōng [鐘] (N) clock; large bell 十点钟 10 o'clock 十分钟 ten minutes	非	fēi * (LC) is not (= 不是) non-; in-; wrong short for Africa 非洲
出	chū * out (directional compl.) (V) to issue; to put up; to produce; to arise	忘	wàng (V) to forget
发	fā [發] (V) to send out; to emit; to develop; to get into a cer- tain state	马	mǎ [馬] (N) horse a surname
刻	kè * moment (M) quarter of an hour (V) to carve; to engrave	毕	bì * [畢] to finish; to accomplish; to conclude
才	cái (A) just; then and only then; not until	业	yè * [業] line of business; industry; occupation; employment; course of study
回	huí (V) to return to; to answer (M) occasion; for affairs, matters	告	gào * to tell, to inform 告诉 (V) to sue
整	zhěng * whole; complete; full; entire; to put in order ; in good order	诉	sù [訴] (V) to tell (in great de- tail); to complain; to appeal
午	wǔ * noon 中午	数	shù [數] (N) number; figure (NU) several
跑	pǎo (V) to run (to); to run about doing sth.; to run away	司	sī * to control; to be in charge of
门	mén [門] (N) door, gate; entrance; gateway (M) for subjects (for study)	专	zhuān [專] (SV) concentrated; special- ized
碰	pèng (V) to touch; to bump; to meet with; to run into	计	jì * [計] to reckon; to compute (N) idea; plan; trick; * stratagem

脑	nǎo　　　　[腦] (N) brain	婚	hūn　　　　* marriage 结婚 (VO) get married
懂	dǒng (V) to understand	候	hòu * time 时候 ; season; in- quire after 问候 (V) to wait （等)候
简	jiǎn　　*　[簡] simple 简单 ; simplified; brief	猜	cāi (V) to guess; to suspect
释	shì　　　*　[釋] to explain 解释 ; to release; to set free	漂	piào　　　　* 漂亮 (SV) elegant; smart; beautiful; handsome
除	chú (V) to deduct; to divide (　　arith.) (CV) apart from	亮	liàng (SV) bright; shiny (N) light, illumination (V) to show
牛	niú (N) cattle, cow　　(M: 头/只) a surname	器	qì implement, untensil, ware, instrument
弹	tán　　　　[弹] (V) to pluck (a string); to flip	差	chà　　　　[差] (V) lack; differ by (SV) short of, not up to the 　　mark
琴	qín (N) the seven-stringed lute; a general name for certain musical instruments	叔	shū/shú (N) uncle (father's younger brother)
自	zì　　　　* self; oneself 自己 ; self- (CV) from; since	爸	bà (N) pa, dad 爸爸 papa
己	jǐ　　　　* oneself; one's own	牌	pái (N) plate, tablet, placard, sign; brand; mahjong piece, dominoes, cards, etc.
结	jié　　　　[結] (V) to tie; to knot; to weave; to congeal		

晨	日 旦 尸 尽 晨 晨 晨
钟	丿 𠂉 午 钅 钌 钟
出	𡶶 山 屮 出 出
发	一 少 发 发 发
刻	亠 亡 方 亥 亥 刻 刻
才	一 十 才
回	丶 冂 回 回
整	敕 三 束 束 敕 敕
	正 一 丁 下 正 正
午	丿 𠂉 二 午
跑	口 卩 𡉉 𧾷 𧾷 跑 跑 跑 跑
门	丶 亠 门
碰	厂 石 石 矿 砰 砰 碰
面	一 丆 厂 丙 而 面 面
非	丿 𠃌 𠄌 丯 非 非 非
忘	亠 亡 忘 忘
马	𠃌 马 马
毕	一 比 比 比 毕 毕
业	丨 川 川 业 业
告	丿 二 牛 生 告
诉	讠 讠 讠 讠 诉 诉
数	娄 丷 丷 米 米 娄 娄
	攵 丿 𠂉 广 攵
司	𠃌 𬱟 司
专	一 二 专 专

计	讠 计 计
脑	月 肸 肸 肢 脑 脑
懂	忄 丨 忄 忄
董	艹 芏 苦 苦 苜 董 董 董
简	竹 ⺮ 竹 竹 简 简
释	釆 丿 乂 丞 丞 釆
	丞 丿 乂 丞 丞 丞
除	𠂤 阝 阝 阽 阽 除 除
牛	丿 𠂉 二 牛
弹	𠃌 𡦳 弓 弓 弹 弹 弹 弹
琴	二 千 王 玨 玨 玨 琴 琴 琴
自	丿 丨 竹 自 自
己	𠃌 𠃍 己
结	纟 纟 纟 纟 结 结 结
婚	乚 乚 女 𡛁 𡛁 娇 婚
候	亻 亻 伫 仴 仴 侯 候
猜	丿 犭 犭 犷 犷 猎 猜
漂	丶 氵 氵 汀 汩 漂 漂
亮	亠 古 古 亨 亮
器	口 哭 哭 哭 器
差	丷 兰 羊 差 差 差
叔	丨 上 卡 朱 叔 叔
爸	丶 八 父 父 谷 爸 爸
牌	片 丿 丿 广 片
卑	丿 丿 冖 𢆲 日 𢆲 里 卑

89

VOCABULARY

早晨 zǎochen (TW) morning

点钟 diǎn zhōng (M-N) hour of the clock

出发 chūfā (V) set out

刻 kè (M) quarter (of an hour)

才 cái (A) only then; not until

回来 huílai (V) come back

回 huí (V) return to

整整 zhěngzhěng (A) fully; a whole

上午 shàngwǔ (TW) morning, a.m.

下午 xiàwǔ (TW) afternoon, p.m.

跑 pǎo (V) to run (to), (hurry) to; run away

分 fēn (M) minute (clock time)

没想到 méi xiǎngdào (IE) unexpectedly, to one's surprise

门口(儿) ménkǒu(r) (PW) entrance

碰见 pèngjiàn (V) run into, meet

见面 jiàn-miàn (V-O) meet, see one another

非常 fēicháng (A) exceptionally

高兴 gāoxìng (SV) pleased, exhilarated

忘(了) wàng(-le) (V) forget

马上 mǎshàng (A) at once (lit. on horseback)

进 jìn (V) enter

酒馆儿 jiǔguǎnr (N) pub

毕业 bì-yè (V-O) to graduate, finish school

以后 yǐhòu (TW) after, afterwards, later

告诉 gàosu (V) tell

数学 shùxué (N) mathematics

家 jiā (M) for families and business establishments

公司 gōngsī (N) company, corporation

专门 zhuānmén (SV/A) special(ly)

电子 diànzǐ (N) electron

计算机 jìsuànjī (N) calculating machine, computer

电脑 diànnǎo (N) 'electric brain'— computer

干 gàn (V) do, work, get on with

懂 dǒng (V) understand

简单 jiǎndān (SV) simple

解释 jiěshì (V) explain

回 huí (M) occasion; for affairs

一回事 yì huí shì (NU-M-N) a matter, business

怎么一回事 zěnme yì huí shì (IE) what it's all about

小时 xiǎoshí (N/M) hour

除了....以外 chúle ....yǐwài (PH) apart from ......

最后 zuìhòu (MA) finally, eventually

只好 zhǐhǎo (A) be forced to, could only

牛 niú (N) cattle, cow

弹琴 tán qín (VO) play/strum lute

钟头 zhōngtóu (N) hour

脑子 nǎozi (N) brain

自己 zìjǐ (PN) oneself

结婚 jié-hūn (V-O) marry

90

时候 shíhou (N) time

   …的时候 …de shíhou (TW) when, while

好 hǎo (SV) be on good terms

分开 fēnkāi (V) separate, part

一起 yìqǐ (A) together

分钟 fēn zhōng (M-N) minute (length of time)

听说 tīngshuō (V/N) hear (it said) that; hearsay

猜 cāi (V) guess

漂亮 piàoliang (SV) pretty, handsome

能干 nénggàn (SV) capable, competent

机器人 jīqìrén (N) mechanical person, robot

   机器 jīqì (N) machine, machinery

出去 chūqu (V) go out

早饭 zǎofàn (N) breakfast

差 chà (V) lack, differ by
   (SV) short of, not up to the mark

   差不多 chàbuduō (SV) almost the same (lit. doesn't differ much)
   (A) almost, about
   (IE) not bad, just about right

叔叔 shūshu (N) uncle (father's younger brother); 'uncle' (polite usage by children)

爸(爸) bà(ba) (N) pa, dad

打牌 dǎ pái (VO) play mahjong or cards

　　昨天我到伦敦去了。早晨八点多钟出发，晚上十一点一刻才回来，整整忙了一天。伦敦人多，车也多，到哪儿去都不容易。从上午十点到下午五点半，我一共跑了八个地方，办了三件大事，饭也没吃，茶也没喝，真是又饿又累。本来打算坐六点零六分的火车回家，没想到在车站门口儿碰见了大学同学小李。老朋友见面当然非常高兴，我也忘了累，马上就跟他进了酒馆儿。每人先喝了三杯，才开始谈毕业以后的情形。他告诉我他先在中学教了一年数学，又在工厂当了两年工人，后来有人介绍他进了现在工作的这家公司，专门搞电子计算机——也就是我们常说的电脑。他对这个工作非常有兴趣，已经干了六、七年了。他知道我完全不懂电脑，就用最简单的数学跟我解释电脑是怎么一回事，可是他说了一个多小时，除了零跟一以外，我还是什么都不懂。最后我只好跟他说：

DIALOGUE

A：小李，你别'对牛弹琴'了，你说了一个多钟头了，我还是不懂，我们谈谈别的吧！

B：谈别的？我搞电脑搞了这么多年了，现在脑子里除了电脑，什么都没有了。

A：谈谈你自己的事吧，先告诉我结婚了没有？

B：还没呢！现在找个对象真不简单，我已经找了几年了。

A：你在大学的时候，不是有个学历史的女朋友吗？

B：你说的是小张吧？是，我们两个人好了五年多，可是我进了电脑公司，她就跟我分开了。

A：为什么？

B：因为我总是跟电脑在一起，每天最多只能跟她见面几分钟。

A：那当然不行！听说电脑也能替人找对象，是真的吗？

B：当然是真的，电脑什么事都能做。有一次我问电脑，象我这样的人应该找什么样的人做对象，你猜电脑说什么？

A：一定说你应该找一位又漂亮、又能干、又......

B：不对，不对，电脑说象我这样儿的人只能找个机器人做对象！

(1) A: 昨天星期天,出去了没有?

B: 出去了.吃了早饭,就到山上去了.

A: 从你家到山上得走几个钟头啊?

B: 我八点十分出发,差一刻十点就到了.走了差不多一个半小时.

A: 真快啊! 天气这么冷,你到山上去干吗?

B: 我去打太极拳.

A: 打太极拳一定要到山上去吗?

B: 不一定,可是教我太极拳的老师在山上.

A: 你学了多久了?

B: 已经学了三年了.

A: 你能不能解释解释'太极'是怎么一回事?

B: 要是我知道'太极'是怎么一回事,我也到山上去了.

(2) A: 张叔叔,您来了.

B: 小胖儿,你爸爸在家吗?

A: 我爸不在家,吃了饭就出去了.

B: 什么时候回来啊?

A: 恐怕得十一点吧.

B: 到哪儿去了?

A: 他没说到哪儿去,可是我知道.

B: 可以告诉我吗?我有事要找他.

A: 告诉您可以,可是您不能告诉我妈.

B: 为什么?

A: 我爸到口儿上那家酒馆儿喝酒去了,我妈最不高兴我爸喝酒了.

B: 你妈也不在家吗?

A: 不在.我妈去打牌去了.可是您别告诉我爸爸,我爸最不高兴我妈打牌了.

(1) Time expressions

(a) Reading of clock time

1:00	一点(钟) / 一点整
2:03	两点(零)三分
3:10 (p.m.)	(下午)三点十分
4:15	四点十五分 / 四点一刻
5:20 (a.m.)	(早晨)五点二十分
6:30	六点三十分 / 六点半
7:40	七点四十分
8:45 (p.m.)	(晚上)八点四十五分 / 八点三刻 / 差一刻九点 / 九点差一刻
9:50 (a.m.)	(上午)九点五十分 / 差十分十点 / 十点差十分
12:55	十二点五十五分 / 差五分一点 / 一点差五分
19:47	十九点四十七分
22:30	二十二点三十分
after 2 p.m. (before 3)	下午两点多(钟)
5 or 6 o'clock	五、六点(钟)
11 or 12 o'clock	十一、二点(钟)

Pattern: Time When   V   (O)

你什么时候去?   我明天上午九点去。

你每天几点钟吃早饭?   八点一刻。

1. 几点了?   快四点了,火车四点几分开?
2. 今天新闻什么时候?   好象是九点十分。
3. 他打算什么时候来?   下午两点。
4. 你每天晚上几点钟睡觉?   最早十一点半。
5. 你坐几点(钟)的车回来?   我坐八点零五分的车回来。
6. 十一点五十五的火车什么时候到?   差五分十二点到。

(b) Length of time in hours and minutes

1 min.	一分钟
15 mins./$\frac{1}{4}$ hour	十五分钟 / 一刻钟
30 mins./$\frac{1}{2}$ hour	三十分钟 / 半(个)小时 / 半个钟头
45 mins./$\frac{3}{4}$ hour	四十五分钟 / 三刻钟
55 mins.	五十五分钟
1 hour	一(个)小时 / 一个钟头
2 hrs.	两(个)小时 / 两个钟头
3 hrs. 2 mins.	三小时零二分
$4\frac{1}{4}$ hrs.	四小时十五分 / 四个钟头(零)一刻钟
$5\frac{1}{2}$ hrs.	五个半小时 / 五个半钟头

Patterns: a.
```
            V  Time How Long
你们要去    多   久      ?
```

b.
```
            V  Time How Long (de) O
他每天看 几个钟头 的 书?
```

or:
```
            V  O,  V Time How Long
他每天看书,看 几个钟头?
```

1. 做这个菜要多少分钟?　　很快,最多五分钟.
2. 今天的新闻长不长?　　不长,只有一刻钟.
3. 从你家到图书馆得坐多久的车?　　差不多七、八分钟.
4. 她想学多久的中文?　　最少四年.
5. 他每天教几个小时的书?　　一、三、五,两小时;二、四,三小时.
6. 你每天打多久的太极拳?　　早晨三刻钟,晚上三刻钟.

(2) <u>Sentence particle 'le' indicating 'accomplished fact'</u>

Patterns: a.
```
              V  O  le ma?
昨天你看电视了吗?
```

b.
```
              V  O (le) méiyou?        V le. or Méi(you) V.
昨天你看电视了  没有?          看了. or 没(有) 看.
```

c.
```
              V méi V  O ?
昨天你看没看电视?
```

95

1. 早晨看报了吗?　　早晨太忙了,没看.有什么新闻?
2. 星期天谁看电影儿了?　　小王看了,我们都没看。
3. 昨天你们在城里买东西了没有?　　没有,我们都没带钱。
4. 那天你也喝酒了吗?　　平常我不喝,可是那天我也喝了。
5. 你在那儿碰见谁了?　　碰见老王了。
6. 昨天下午你没写汉字吗?　　没有,我出去了。
7. 她已经到日本了吗?　　早就到了。
8. 去年他学中文没有?　　学了。
9. 他还没解释那个问题吗?　　解释了,可是我还是不清楚。

(3) Verb-suffix '-le' for 'completed action'

(a) V-le O as a full sentence

1. 他们两个人见面以后,没说话就进了酒馆儿。
2. 他介绍了这本新书,也解释了电脑替人工作的问题。
3. 大家都说应该请他,所以我们就请了他。
4. 中学毕业以后,他就进了工厂。
5. 我告诉他以后,他马上就告诉了小王。
6. 他们经过了德国、法国,最后到了英国。
7. 除了英文以外,他还学习了历史跟地理。
8. 他弟弟十六岁就当了解放军。

(b) Quantified object

Patterns: a.　　　　V-le NU M　O
　　　　我昨天 跑了 三个 地方。
　　　b.　　　　V-le Time How Long (de)　O
　　　　他昨天 坐了 八个钟头　的 飞机。
　　　c.　　　　V O,　V-le Time How Long
　　　　他昨天 坐飞机, 坐了　八个钟头。

1. 你买了几张票?　　我买了三张票。
2. 昨天晚上你写了多少个汉字?　　我一共写了两百四十五个。
3. 他在这儿的时候,你们吃了几次中国饭?　　三次。

96

4. 她去年在中国学了一点儿中文． 现在都忘了吧．

5. 我昨天只睡了四个钟头,今天非常累．

6. 他都去了哪些国家？ 他去了法国、德国、苏联跟美国．

7. 中学毕业以后,他没进大学,当了几年售货员．

8. 星期六你打了一天牌吧？ 没有,我只打了三个钟头．

9. 昨天他念了几个钟头的书？ 他只念了五分钟．

10. 今天我坐了一上午的汽车． 你到哪儿去了？

11. 她在这儿一共只学了三个星期的英文．

12. 今天早晨老师没来,我们就谈了两个钟头的天儿．

(c) V-le O as a dependent clause

Pattern: V-le (O), Main clause

看了 朋友， 去吃饭．

1. 你什么时候去？ 我吃了饭,马上就去．

2. 他回去了吗？ 回去了,吃了饭就回去了．

3. 我现在可以去玩儿吗？ 不行,你得写了字才能去玩儿．

4. 票买了吗？ 还没呢,我打算看了老李就去买．

5. 他每天什么时候打太极拳？ 他吃了早饭就打．

6. 你很累吗？ 不累,只是喝了酒,很想睡觉．

7. 你们什么时候来？ 看了电影来,行不行？

8. 你给他的信写了吗？ 写了,昨天客人走了,我就写了．

9. 他们结了婚,想到中国去．

10. 她学了三天,就不想学了．

11. 他们走了五分钟,我才回来．

12. 这本数学太难了,我看了很久,还是不懂．

(4) Combination of verb-suffix '-le' and sentence particle 'le'

(a) Where the verb ends the sentence or clause, and le might serve a double function

1. 他来了吗？ 他早就来了．

2. 去北京的那四个人都回来了吗?
   两个回来了,两个还没回来呢.

3. 你想吃什么?我给你做. 我已经吃了,别给我做了.

4. 他们还在一起吗? 已经分开了.

5. 老师叫你写的字,写了没有? 还没呢,我忘了.

6. 他请你办的那件事,你办了没有? 办了,我已经告诉他了.

(b) Where the suffix -le is included before a simple object only if
completion of the action is stressed

1. 你们都吃(了)饭了吗? 都吃了,一个钟头以前就吃了.

2. 给老王介绍个女朋友吧.
   他已经有(了)对象了,你别替他着急了.

3. 她们怎么还没来?你请(了)她们了吗?
   请了,她们说马上就来.

4. 他今年还不到四十岁,可是两个女儿都进(了)大学了.

5. 十天前他就到(了)伦敦了. 怎么没人告诉我啊?

6. 别看电影儿了,我请你吃饭去.
   不行,我已经买(了)票了,不能不看.

(c) Progress up to the present

Patterns: a.　　V -le NU M (O) le
　　　　　　　我 喝 了 五杯 　了,不能再喝了.

　　　　b.　　V -le Time How Long (de) O le
　　　　　　　他 写 了 四个多钟头 的 汉字了,真想去睡觉.

　　　or　　V O,　V -le Time How Long le
　　　　　　　他 写汉字,写 了 四个多钟头 了,真想去睡觉.

1. 我今天已经写了五百个字了,不能再写了. (or:还得再写五百.)

2. 他已经吃了五个苹果了,还想再吃一个.

3. 他写的那本书,你看了多少了? 已经看了一半了.

4. 什么地方都没有这种酒,我已经跑了八个酒馆儿了.

98

5. 我问了三个人了,都说不知道那家电脑公司在哪儿。
6. 这个电影儿他已经看了三次了,你还想请他看吗?
7. 我在这儿已经坐了三个钟头了,得走了。
8. 这条路真长,我走了一个多小时了,才走了一半。
9. 他在这个单位已经干了二十五年了,很想到别的单位去。
10. 王先生教书教了十八年了,他自己也不知道一共教了多少学生。
11. 我们已经学了十个星期的中文了,有人还想学,有人已经不想学了。

(5) Where verb-suffix '-le' is not used

1. 以前他每年都要到中国去(X)三次。 (habitual activity)
    Contrast: 他去年到中国去了三次。
2. 去年他们找(X)我教了三个星期的外语。 (pivotal construction)
3. 那天他去(X)城里买了不少东西。 (verbal expressions in series)
4. 我早晨去看(X)他的时候,他说(X):"要是你昨天来....."
    (direct speech)
5. 我早晨去看(X)他的时候,他说(X)要是我昨天去.....
    (indirect speech)
6. 昨天他觉得(X)不太舒服,今天已经好了。 (dispositional verb)
7. 我们昨天决定(X)明天早晨出发。 (verbal construction as object)

(6) Specific relative time

Patterns: a. ...yǐqián (before, ago)   三年以前,没人知道这个名字。
          b. ...de shíhou (while, when)   他来的时候,我们都不在家。
          c. ...yǐhòu (after)   解放以后,他就到了我们单位。

1. 到中国去以前,最好学点儿中文。
2. 他每天晚上睡觉以前,都要看半个钟头的小说。
3. 三个星期以前,我在朋友家认识了一位专门搞电脑的华侨。

4. 你们做中国菜的时候，别忘了告诉我。

5. 没事的时候，他就喜欢弹琴。

6. 四年以后你们都能毕业吗？毕业以后打算干什么呢？

7. 这个问题经过他解释以后，我们都很清楚了。

8. 见面以后我才知道她那么难看，真没想到。

9. 这个菜太好吃了！没吃以前想吃，吃了以后更想吃！

10. 结婚以前她说什么他都说行，结婚以后她说什么他都说不行。

(7) Inclusiveness and exclusiveness (with question words as indefinites)

Pattern: 你想吃什么？　a. 我什么都想吃。

　　　　　　　　　　　b. 我什么都/也不想吃。

1. 他要买什么？　a. 他什么都要买。　b. 他什么都不要买。

2. 谁认识这个人？　a. 谁都认识。　b. 谁都不认识。

3. 你想到哪儿去旅行？　a. 我哪儿都想去。　b. 哪儿都可以。

　　　　　　　　　　　c. 除了中国，我哪儿也不想去。

4. 他说我们哪天可以出发？　a. 他说哪天都行。

　　　　　　　　　　　　　b. 他说哪天都不行，他不准我们去。

5. 昨天晚上你做什么了？　a. 我没做什么，看了两个钟头的电视。

　　　　　　　　　　　　b. 什么都没做，看了两个钟头的电视。

6. 电脑能替人做什么？
　除了不能替人吃饭睡觉以外，什么都能做。

7. 她会做鱼吗？　a. 会，她怎么做都好吃。

　　　　　　　　b. 不会，她怎么做都不好吃。

8. 你懂了吗？　这个问题太难了，他怎么解释我都不懂。

(8) 'Jiù' and 'cái' contrasted
(note that 'cai' does not normally combine with 'le')

1a. 他九点钟就来了，太早了。

　b. 他十点半才来，太晚了。

2a. 他说行就行.

　b. 他说行才行.

3a. 我们人少, 三瓶差不多就够了.

　b. 我们人多, 三十瓶才够.

4a. 这条路很近, 我们走了十分钟就到了.

　b. 这条路不近, 我们走了四十分钟才到.

5a. 见面以前, 我就猜她很漂亮.

　b. 见面以后, 我才知道她很漂亮.

6a. 我们到了那儿, 不到一分钟他就来了.

　b. 我们到了那儿, 等了一刻钟他才来.

7a. 这件事很简单, 他就能办. (他不太能干.)

　b. 这件事很不简单, 她才能办. (她非常能干.)

8a. 他吃了半碗就饱了.

　b. 他吃了五碗还不饱.

　c. 他吃了八碗才饱.

9a. 老李还没走吧? 　 走了, 昨天就走了.

　b. 老李已经走了吧? 　 还没呢, 他明天才走.

(9) 'Yǐjing ... le' versus 'hái bù/méi ... ne'

1. 你们都懂了吧?
   他们已经懂了, 我的脑子不行, 还不懂呢.

2. 这些机器你们都会用了吗?
   简单的已经会了, 难的还不太会呢.

3. 你们都吃了吗?
   他们三个已经吃了, 我们两个还没吃呢.

4. 客人都来了吗?
   男的都已经来了, 女的都还没来呢.

5. 他们六个人去了没有？

三个已经到了,两个在路上,一个还没出发呢。

6. 他们都回来了吗？

去北京的早就回来了,去上海的还没回来呢。

7. 你给家里的信都写了吗？

给父亲的已经写了,给叔叔的还没写呢。

8. 这四个姐妹都结婚了吗？

老大、老三,已经结了;老二、老四,还没呢。

(10) 'Chúle ... (yǐwài)', apart from

1. 除了数学,他对什么都没兴趣。
2. 他说的中国话,除了他自己以外,没人懂。
3. 除了学习中文以外,我们还得学习中国历史。
4. 他除了喝酒以外,也喜欢打牌。
5. 除了卖房子以外,没有别的法子吗？

附	fù * to be attached, added, enclosed	望	wàng * [望] to look towards; (to) hope
园	yuán * [園] garden 公园 park; 果园 orchard	将	jiāng [將] (LC) to take (A) to be about to 将来 (in the) future
片	piàn (M) stretch, expanse; slice, thin piece	月	yuè * moon 月亮 (N/M) month 三月 March; 三个月 3 months
林	lín * woods, grove (树)林子 a surname	课	kè [課] (N) subject; course; class (M) lesson
治	zhì * to govern; to manage; to control (V) to heal, treat	录	lù [錄] (V) to record, to tape-record * record; register
医	yī [醫] (N) medical science (V) to give medical treatment	休	xiū * to cease; to rest
院	yuàn * court; institution 院子 courtyard 医院 hospital; 学院 college	息	xī, xí * to rest 休息 ; to cease breathe
大	dài * 大夫 (medical) doctor	复	fù * [復] again, anew; to recover; to review/revise (lessons)复习
流	liú (V) to flow	心	xīn (N) heart; mind; feeling; intention; centre, core
练	liàn [練] (V) to drill, to practise	班	bān (N/M) class (of students); schedule of bus, train or plane; shift of work
功	gōng (N) merit; achievement; skill 功夫 'kung fu'	正	zhèng (SV) right, upright, obverse (A) just right; to be on the point of ....-ing 正要
希	xī * rare; infrequent; to hope	忽	hū * suddenly 忽然 ; to neglect

刚	gāng　　　[剛] * hard, strong (A) just; only just 刚才 just now, a moment ago	州	zhōu (N/M) old administrative region 广州 Guangzhou Canton City
校	xiào　　　* school, college	住	zhù (V) to live (at), to reside * to stop
食	shí　　　* food (LC) to eat	船	chuán (N) boat, ship　　(M:只)
堂	táng * hall (M) for teaching period	句	jù * sentence (M) for words, sentences, lines of verse
戴	dài (V) to wear, to put on (hat, gloves, trappings, glasses, etc.)　　a surname	运	yùn　　　[運] (V) to move about; to transport 运气 (good) luck
表	biǎo　　　[錶] (N) watch　　(M:块/只)	骑	qí　　　[騎] (V) to ride; to sit on the back of
概	gài　　*　[槪] in general, approximate 大概 general idea; on the whole; probably	借	jiè (V) to borrow; to lend 借给
号	hào　　*　[號] (ordinal) number; day of month; date; name; mark 一月四号 Jan. 4	辆	liàng　　　[輛] (M) for vehicles

STROKE—ORDER

附　3 阝 阝 阝 附 附	流　氵 氵 氵 汸 浐 浐 流 流
园　丨 冂 冂 冃 冃 园 园	练　纟 纟 纟 纟 纩 纩 练 练
片　丿 丿 丿 片	功　一 丅 工 巧 功
林　木 林	希　丿 乄 兰 羊 者 希
治　氵 氵 汄 治	望　胡　亠 亡 玎 玥
医　一 厂 匚 三 夨 夨 医	王　一 二 干 王
院　阝 阝 阝 阝 阵 阵 院 院	将　丶 丬 丬 丬 丬 护 护 将 将
大　一 十 大	月　丿 刀 月 月

课　　讠　讥　讠　讠　课　课　课
录　　フ　ヨ　彐　寻　寻　录　录
休　　亻　什　休　休
息　　丿　亻　竹　自　自　息
复　　丿　亠　旨　复　复　复
心　　丶　心　心　心
班　　二　干　王　王　豣　班　班　班
正　　一　丁　下　正　正
忽　　丿　勹　匆　匆　忽
刚　　丨　门　冈　冈　刚　刚
校　　木　朾　栌　栌　栌　校
食　　人　全　今　今　拿　食　食　食
堂　　丨　丬　业　业　屵　峃　堂　堂　堂

戴　　十　吉　击　壴　壴　壹　戴　戴
表　　二　キ　主　丰　未　表　表
概　　木　朾　栌　栌　根　根　椎　椎　概　概
号　　口　吕　号
州　　丶　ノ　小　州　州　州
住　　亻　亻　住　住　住
船　　丿　ソ　月　舟　舟　舟　舩　船
句　　丿　勹　句
运　　一　二　云　云　运
骑　　フ　马　马　驭　驮　骑　骑　骑
借　　亻　亻　借　借　借
辆　　车　一　士　车　车
两　　一　厂　冋　丙　丙　两　两

VOCABULARY

过　guò (V) pass, cross, go through
(V suffix) 'experiential' suffix

附近　fùjìn (PW) vicinity, near by

公园(儿)　gōngyuán(r) (N/PW) park, public gardens

片　piàn (M) stretch, expanse; slice, thin piece

树林子　shùlínzi (N) woods, grove

中午　zhōngwǔ (TW) noon

看到　kàndào (V) see, catch sight of

东方　dōngfāng (PW) orient(al)

一边儿…一边儿…　yìbiānr… yìbiānr…(C)
on the one hand… on the other hand…(reducible to biān…biān… with monosyllabic verbs)

三明治　sānmíngzhì (N) sandwich

别人　biéren (N) other people, others

医院　yīyuàn (N/PW) hospital

有名　yǒu-míng (SV) famous

大夫　dàifu (N) medical doctor

上(大,中,小)学　shàng (dà-,zhōng-,xiǎo-) xué (VO) attend school

从来　cónglái (A) (t)hitherto, up till now/then

从来不 V　never
从来没 V 过　never

不过　búguò (C) however, nevertheless

流利　liúlì (SV) fluent

练　liàn (V) practise, train (in)

功夫　gōngfu (N) skill, art, 'kung fu'; labour, effort

希望　xīwàng (V/N) hope

105

将来 jiānglái (TW) in future

前年 qiánnián (TW) year before last

月 yuè (N) month

一月 二月 ...yī yuè, èr yuè, etc. (TW) January, February, etc.

又 yòu (A) then again; (do sth.) further; go on to (do sth.); on top of that

课 kè (M) lesson

录 lù (V) record

录音 lù-yīn (V-O) 'record sound'; (make a) recording

练习 liànxí (V) practise, drill (N) exercise, practice

休息 xiūxi (V) rest, take a break

复习 fùxí (V) revise (N) revision

用功 yònggōng (SV) diligent, industrious (in one's studies)

心 xīn (N) heart; mind

上星期五 shàng xīngqī-wǔ (TW) last Friday

班 bān (N/M) shift, duty; class (of students)

下班 xià bān (VO) come off duty

正 zhèng (SV/A) straight, right; just, precisely

正要 zhèngyào (A) just about to

忽然 hūrán (MA) suddenly

午饭 wǔfàn (N) lunch

请 qǐng (polite) (IE) please (go ahead, indulge)

刚才 gāngcái (TW) just now, a moment ago

学校 xuéxiào (N) school, college

食堂 shítáng (N) refectory, canteen

戴 dài (V) wear, put on (hat, gloves, trappings, etc.)

表 biǎo (N) watch

大概 dàgài (MA) probably; in general

进来 jìnlai (V) come in

钟 zhōng (N) clock

一会儿 yíhuìr (TW) a short while (also yìhuǐr)

上课 shàng kè (VO) start class; attend class

饭馆儿 fànguǎnr (N)
馆子 guǎnzi (N) } restaurant

下馆子 xià guǎnzi (VO) go to a restaurant

上(个)月 shàng (ge) yuè (TW) last month

号 hào (N) number; day of month

广州 Guǎngzhōu (PW) Canton City

来信 lái xìn (VO) send ('make come') a letter; incoming letter

住 zhù (V) live, stay, reside

下(个)月 xià (ge) yuè (TW) next month

学生 xuésheng (N) student, pupil

船 chuán (N) boat, ship

北方人 běifāng rén (N) northerner

办法 bànfǎ (N) way, means, method

句 jù (M) for words, sentences

运气 yùnqi (N) luck (good or bad)

骑 qí (V) ride

自行车 zìxíngchē (N) bicycle

刚 gāng (A) just, only just

飞 fēi (V) fly

借 jiè (V) borrow, lend

辆 liàng (M) for vehicles

北海公园 Běihǎi Gōngyuán (PW) (north lake) park in Peking

你去过大学附近的那个公园儿吗?里头除了有一片树林子以外,还有一个小湖.去过的人都说那儿的风景不错.中午天气好的时候,我们常常看到一位东方人坐在湖边儿的椅子上,一边儿看书,一边儿吃三明治.这位先生不是别人,他就是大学医院很有名的王大夫.王大夫的父母都是中国人,可是他是在英国生的,小学、中学、大学也都是在英国上的,从来没到过中国.不过他能说很流利的广东话,也练过几种功夫,那都是小时候他父亲教他的.他很希望将来有机会到中国去工作,所以前年九月又开始学习普通话,到现在已经学了快两年了.他没有中文老师,是自己学的.一个星期最少学一课.每天早晨听录音,晚上练习汉字.中午休息的时候还要到湖边儿去复习,非常用功.好象他一天不学中文,心里就不舒服.上星期五中午下班以后,他买了两块三明治,又到了湖边儿,正要开始边吃边看的时候,忽然后头有人叫他:

DIALOGUE

A:王大夫,您好啊!这儿风景真不错!

B:欸!小李,是你啊,吃午饭了吗?我这儿有三明治。

A:您请吧,我吃了,刚才在学校食堂吃的.噢,对不起,请问您现在几点了?我没戴表。

B:现在是……欸?我的表大概忘在医院了,不过我刚才进来的时候门口的大钟还不到一点半。

A:那好,我还可以再休息一会儿.我们两点才上课呢.王大夫,您好象很久没到我们饭馆儿来了,天天吃三明治怎么行啊?

B:最近太忙了,已经有两、三个月没下过馆子了.家里人都好吧?

A：都好.我父亲回中国去了,您知道吗?

B：我没听说啊,是什么时候走的?要去多久啊?

A：他是上月二十三号上的飞机,二十五号晚上到的广州,现在住在我叔叔家.昨天来信说恐怕下个月才能回来.

B：他以前回去过吗?

A：三十年前他做学生的时候回去过一次,那次是坐船回去的,在路上整整走了一个月.

B：欸,小李,你不是在英国生的吗?怎么能说这么流利的普通话?在哪儿学的?

A：我们从小在家就说普通话.我妈是北方人,不会说广东话,也没学过英文,所以我们都跟她说普通话.

B：你们真好!现在很多华侨家里都说英文,忘了自己是从哪儿来的.你想想:中国人不会说中国话怎么行啊?

A：我们开始上小学以后,也常常在家里说英文,可是我母亲想了一个好办法,叫我们一定得说中国话.

B：什么好办法?

A：很简单:谁说中国话她就给谁吃中国饭;谁说英文她就给谁吃三明治.我们都怕吃三明治,所以现在才都能说几句中国话.

B：你们运气真好.我现在天天练习说中国话,可是还得在这儿吃三明治!

SKETCHES

(1) A：你见过我的朋友李大明吗？

B：没见过,不过好象听你说过这个人。

A：有机会我可以给你们介绍介绍,这个人你应该认识认识。

B：为什么？

A：这个人非常不简单,他来英国以前在中国学过数学,办过工厂,搞过新闻,还写过三本小说。

B：真的吗？到英国以后他做过什么事？

A：他进过工厂,当过售货员,学过历史,教过太极拳,去年又开始搞电脑……

B：这个人真行,我从来没听说过有这么能干的人,他现在在哪儿工作啊？

A：进了医院了。

B：噢,当了大夫了？

A：不是,不是大夫说他的脑子得休息休息!

(2) A：刚才骑自行车来的那个中国学生是谁？

B：他姓牛,刚从上海来的,现在就住在我那儿。

A：你是在哪儿认识他的？

B：我们是前年在北京认识的。

A：我不知道你最近回过中国,一个人去的吗？

B：不是,我是跟两个朋友一起去的。

A：从这儿到北京你们飞了多少个小时？

B：我们不是坐飞机去的,飞机票太贵了,我们是坐火车去的。

A：你们在北京都看了些什么地方啊？

B：太多了,我们三个人借了三辆自行车,天天骑车出去玩儿,那些有名的地方我们差不多都去了。

A：真的？能不能说说给我们听听？

B：没问题,可是不知道你们有没有时间,因为只说北海公园恐怕我就得说一晚上。

SPEECH PATTERNS

(1) <u>Verbal suffix '-guo' as a sign for the indefinite past</u>

Patterns: a.   V <u>-guo</u>   O   <u>ma</u>?

你坐过飞机吗?

      b.   V <u>-guo</u>   O   <u>méiyou</u>?   V <u>-guo</u>./ <u>Méi</u> V <u>-guo</u>

你坐过飞机没有?   坐过. / 没坐过.

      c.   V (<u>-guo</u>) <u>méi</u>(<u>you</u>) V <u>-guo</u> O ?

你坐(过) 没(有) 坐过飞机?

1. 你吃过中国饭没有?   吃过,我常吃.
2. 你去过广州吗?   去过,小时候跟父母去过一次.
3. 您以前来过伦敦吗?   没来过,这是第一次.
4. 你听说过这种电脑吗?   听说过,我们公司用的就是这种.
5. 这本小说你没看过吗?   没看过,我不太喜欢看历史小说.
6. 他练过多久的功夫?   一共练过八个月.
7. 你从来不看中国电影吗?

很少看,在中国二十年我只看过一回.

8. 你好象从来没喝过这么多酒.

是啊,因为我从来没这么高兴过.

9. 最近你们那儿天气怎么样?   上星期冷过两天,这星期不错.
10. 她一直这么瘦吗?   是啊,她从来没胖过.
11a. 最近我去看过她两次.

   b. 最近我看过两次中国电影.

(2) <u>Verb '-le' and verb '-guo' contrasted</u>

1a. 老李去不去?   <u>他以前去过</u>,不想再去了.

   b. 老王去不去?   <u>他已经去了</u>.

2a. <u>他到中国去过</u>,知道一点儿中国的情形.

   b. <u>他到中国去了</u>,大概下月十五号才能回来.

3a. <u>他当过解放军</u>,现在是公社干部.

   b. <u>他当了解放军</u>,身体更好了.

110

4a. 没想到他碰见了这种事,你说怎么办?
 b. 老李碰见过这种事,他知道应该怎么办。
5a. 我买过一本他写的小说,现在不知道到哪儿去了。
 b. 我买了一本他写的小说,打算在船上看。
6a. 他没喝过中国茶,当然不知道中国茶怎么样。
 b. 昨天他没喝中国茶,只喝了一杯咖啡。

(3) 'Zai' used as verb complement

Pattern: V<u>zai</u>   O
            您住在 哪儿? 我住在伦敦。

1. 那边儿人多,我们就坐在这儿休息休息吧。
2. 我们怎么走?
   你别怕,我走在你前头,他跟在你后头,你走在中间儿,行不行?
3. 很多没有家的人晚上睡在火车站。
4. 他们两个人坐在公园儿的椅子上,又吃又喝。
5. 别人都有书,你怎么没书? 我也有,可是忘在家里了。
6. 小孩子坐汽车的时候都喜欢坐在前头。
7. 你看我这个东西戴在这儿好不好看? 戴在哪儿都不好看。
8. 他(是)哪儿人? 他生在北京,可是小学、中学都是在上海念的。
9. 名字写在什么地方? 就写在里头吧。
10. 他们五个人住在一起,三个住在前头,两个住在后头。
11. 你的时间应该用在听录音上,不应该用在听音乐上。
12. 他们两个人走在树林子里,一边儿谈天儿,一边儿看风景。
13. 生活在今天的英国,你觉得有希望吗?
14. 那天运气真不好,我在路上走,忽然一个东西打在我的头上....

(4) Place as adverbial compared with place as complement
(∼ = similar to, ≠ = distinct from)

1a. 您住在哪儿? ∼ b. 您在哪儿住?
2a. 我们坐在外边儿吧。 ∼ b. 我们在外边儿坐吧。

111

3a. 他天天睡在公园儿里。～ b. 他天天在公园儿里睡。

4a. 请你写在桌子上。≠ b. 请你在桌子上写。

5a. 表不能戴在这儿。≠ b. 在这儿不能戴表。

6a. 录在哪儿？≠ b. 在哪儿录？

(5) <u>'Shi ... de' construction to bring out attendant circumstances</u>

(a) Without object

Patterns: a.　　(shi)　Time　V　de
　　　　　　　他 是 什么时候 来 的？　是上个月来的。
　　　　　b.　(shi)　Place　V　de
　　　　　　　他 是 从哪儿 来 的？　是从中国来的。
　　　　　c.　(shi)　Means　V　de
　　　　　　　他 是 怎么 来 的？　是坐飞机来的。

1. 你叔叔是什么时候走的？　是上星期三走的。

2. 你不是去年九月来的吗？　不是，我是去年八月来的。

3. 这些人都是从苏联来的吗？
　 一半是从苏联来的，一半是从东德来的。(东德，'East Germany')

4. 他是不是在英国生的？
　 不是，不过小学、中学都是在英国上的。

5. 你这件毛衣真漂亮，在哪儿买的？
　 不漂亮，就是在我家附近的那个商店买的。

6. 你们是在哪儿碰见的？　在北京车站门口儿，没想到吧。

7. 今天你们是怎么来的？　他们是走路来的，我是骑车来的。

8. 老王是怎么去的？　他是坐船去的。

9. 你是不是跟他一起来的？　不是，我是自己一个人来的。

10. 她是一九七几年毕业的？　她是七七年毕业的。

(b) With object

Patterns: a.　　(shi)　Time　　V　O(PN)　de
　　　　　　　他 是什么时候去找你 的？　上星期六早晨。
　　　　　b.　(shi) Place V de　O
　　　　　　　你 是在哪儿吃的午饭？　在学生食堂吃的。

1. 你是去年几月碰见他的？

112

好象是六月,就在北海公园儿门口儿.

2. 你是在哪儿认识她的? 我们是在公安局认识的.

3. 他是哪天给你的钱? 忘了,不是星期六就是星期五.

4. 你是什么时候买的票?

昨天下班以后买的,是跟朋友借的钱.

5. 你叔叔是哪年去的美国? 就是我生的那年.

6. 他们是几月几号结的婚? 六月十五号.

7. 你们是不是昨天做的练习? 不是我们是上星期四做的.

8. 你是在哪儿买的自行车?

就在我们工厂附近的那家百货公司.

9. 你今天几点钟听的录音?

中午十二点听的,整整听了一个钟头.

10. 你们是怎么去的医院? 坐朋友的车去的.

11. 是谁说的我的中文没希望了? 是别人说的,不是我.

12. 是谁告诉你的他从来不抽烟? 是他自己告诉我的.

13a. 我下午没出去,我(是)早晨买的菜.

 b. 你看,这就是我早晨买的菜.

14. 他是昨天来的. ≠ 他(就)是昨天来的(那个)人.

(6) Verb '-le'/verb '-guo' contrasted with 'shi ... de'

1a. 我去过海德公园. ('Hyde Park')
 b. 你是什么时候去的?

2a. 老李到法国去了.
 b. 他是怎么去的?

3a. 老王已经坐船走了.
 b. 他是在哪儿上的船?

4a. 他们已经结婚了.
 b. 是几月结的?在哪儿结的?

5a. 我昨天买了一个小钟.
 b. 你是跟谁一起去买的?

6a. 她以前学过三年中文.

b. 她是用什么法子学的?

7a. 他上过大学.

b. 他是哪年毕业的?

8a. 昨天我做了两百块三明治.

b. 你是替谁做的?

(7) <u>Time elapsed and time within which</u>

Patterns: a. 他一天听半小时的录音.

b. 他一天没听录音.

1. 他一个星期不学汉字,就不舒服.

   cf. 他一个星期学两百个汉字.

2. 她一个星期没学汉字. cf. 她一个星期学了两百个汉字.

3. 去年他差不多(有)三个月没工作. cf. 去年他工作了三个月.

4. 我已经(有)十年没说法文了,完全都忘了.

5. 我很久没给他写信了,不知道他最近怎么样.

6. 买了汽车以后,他已经(有)两年没骑自行车了.

7. 她去年在中国,三个月没说过半句英文.

8. 他已经三天没喝酒了,当然没有什么精神了.

9a. 她练习了两年.

b. 她没练习两年,只练习了一年半.

c. 她两年没练习了.

10a. 他坐了三天的汽车.

b. 他没坐三天(的汽车),只坐了两天.

c. 他三天没坐汽车.

(8) <u>Verbs of locomotion</u>

1. 上山 / 下山   上山容易,下山难.

114

2. 上车 / 下车　　你是在哪儿上的车？打算在哪站下车？

3. 上飞机 / 下飞机　　这些人是要上飞机的,那些人是刚下飞机的。

4. 上哪儿？　　他上哪儿了？

5. 上馆子 or 下馆子　　他们有钱,常常下馆子。

6. 上学　　孩子们早晨七点上学。

　　　　他才四岁,还没上学呢。

　　　　他将来希望到外国去上大学。

7. 上课 / 下课　　我们学校九点钟开始上课。

　　　　时间到了,老师忘了下课。

8. 进城 / 出城　　早晨进城的人多,晚上出城的人多。

9. 回家　　下了课,我得马上骑车回家。

(9) Verbs of motion compounded with 'lai' and 'qu'

1. 进来　　外头那么冷,你为什么不进来？
   进去　　里头人太多,我不想进去。

2. 出来　　你出来看看,外头真漂亮。
   出去　　你出去看看,外头好象有人说话。

3. 回来　　已经十二点了,他怎么还没回来,我不等他了。
   回去　　已经十二点了,我得回去了,再见！

4. 上来　　山上风景真好,你们都上来吧。
   上去　　我太累了,我不上去,我在这儿等你们。

5. 下来　　山上太冷了,你们下来吧。
   下去　　你们先下去,我马上就来。

6. 买来　　菜已经买来了。
   买去　　他买去的书都是没人要的。

7. 送来　　电视机已经买了,明天送来。（电视机，'T.V. set'）
   送去　　他要看这本书,你给他送去好吧？

8. 过来　　请你过来看看这是什么。
   过去　　请你过去跟他们说,请他们过来谈谈。

楼	lóu [樓] (N) storied building 三楼 3rd floor (British second)	慢	màn (SV) slow
妇	fù * [婦] woman 妇女 women (as a class)	连	lián [連] (V) to join (CV) even (including) 连…也/都
兄	xiōng * elder brother	较	jiào [較] * to compare (A) comparatively; fairly; quite
俩	liǎ [倆] (NU+M) two (fusion of 两 and 个)	了	liǎo (V) to finish; to conclude 不得了 (SV) awful, terrible (SV comp) awfully
脸	liǎn [臉] (N) face	唱	chàng (V) to sing
眼	yǎn (N) eye 眼睛 (M: 只 & 双)	歌	gē (N) song (LC) to sing 国歌 national anthem
睛	jīng * eyeball	离	lí [離] (V) to leave (a place) (CV) (distant) from
长	zhǎng [長] (V) to grow * elder; senior; head; chief 校长 headmaster, principal	好	hào (V) to be fond of, to be fond of …-ing
比	bǐ (V) to compare (CV) compared with short for Belgium 比利时	奇	qí (SV) peculiar; rare; wonderful
双	shuāng [雙] (M) pair of, couple of *two; twin; dual; double	各	gè (SP) each; various
聪	cōng * [聰] (LC) faculty of hearing; acute (of hearing) 聪明 intelligent, clever	怪	guài (SV) strange; odd; queer (V) to blame
性	xìng * * quality; nature; character (N) sex 男/女性 the male/female sex	答	dá (V) to answer, to reply 回答 (V/N) answer, reply

雨	yǔ (N) rain 下雨 (VO) to rain	关	guān　　　　　[關] (V) to shut, close; to turn off (N) pass; barrier
窗	chuāng (N) window 窗户／窗子	系	xì　　　*　　[係] (LC) is; is of the nature of 关系 relation(ship); relevance
户	hù * door (M) a household	木	mù　　　　* wood, trees (AT) wooden
糊	hú　　　　* paste; to stick with paste	意	yì　　　　* idea; meaning 意思; intention 有(没)意思 be (un)interesting
涂	tú　　　　[塗] (V) to spread; to smear; to scribble 糊涂 muddled; confused	思	sī　　　　* to think; to long for 思想 thought, thinking
麻	má (N) hemp (SV) numb; insensitive	白	bái (SV) white; plain; fair, pale (of complexion)
烦	fán　　　　[煩] (SV) be vexed; be annoyed (V) to bother 麻烦 trouble; troublesome	嘴	zuǐ　　　　[嘴] (N) mouth　　　　(M:张)
记	jì　　　　[記] (V) to memorize; to remember; to record (N) mark; sign	笨	bèn (SV) stupid; obtuse; clumsy
首	shǒu * head; beginning; first (M) for songs and poems		

STROKE-ORDER

楼　木 杧 栌 栌 栏 楼 楼 楼 楼	睛　月 月 肝 胪 晴 睛 睛
妇　く 女 女 如 妇 妇	长　丿 一 长 长
兄　口 尸 兄	比　一 比 比 比
俩　亻 仁 仃 伓 俩 俩 俩 俩	双　丁 又 双 双
脸　月 月 肸 脸 脸 脸 脸 脸	聪　一 厂 耳 耳 耳 耶 聊 聪
眼　刂 月 目 肝 眼 眼 眼 眼 眼	性　丨 忄 忄 忄 忙 忙 性 性

117

慢　忄 忄 悍 悍 愠 慢 慢
连　一 七 七 车 连
较　一 七 车 车 轩 轩 较 较
了　了 了
唱　口 叩 唱
歌　哥 可 哥 哥 歌 歌 歌
离　一 亠 文 立 卤 卤 离 离 离
好　く 女 女 奵 奵 好
奇　一 十 大 达 吞 奇 奇
各　ノ ク 久 各
怪　忄 忄 怌 怪 怪 怪
答　⺮ ⺮ 竹 笠 笑 答
雨　一 厂 冂 雨 雨 雨
窗　一 穴 宀 宛 窈 窗 窗
户　丶 ㇆ ㇕ 户

糊　⺷ ⺷ 半 半 米 籿 粘 糊 糊
涂　氵 汋 泠 涂 涂 涂
麻　广 广 床 麻
烦　丷 少 火 灯 炻 烦 烦
记　讠 记 记 记
首　丷 ⺌ 艹 芦 首 首
关　丷 兰 关 关
系　一 ㇈ 幺 幺 乎 系 系
木　一 十 才 木
意　亠 立 立 音 意
思　冂 田 冊 田 思
曰　ノ 亻 冂 勹 曰
嘴　口 口 叶 叶 吣 吣 吡 吡 嘴 嘴 嘴
　嘴
笨　⺮ ⺮ 竺 竿 笨 笨 笨

VOCABULARY

楼　lóu (N) storied building
　　(M) floor
　三楼　sān lóu (PW) 3rd floor (
　　British second)
　楼上　lóu-shàng (PW) upstairs
　楼下　lóu-xià (PW) downstairs
夫妇　fūfù (N) husband and wife,
　　married couple
兄弟　xiōngdì (N) brothers; younger
　　brother
俩　liǎ (N+M) two (= liǎng ge)
脸　liǎn (N) face
眼睛　yǎnjing (N) eye
长　zhǎng (V) grow
得　de (K) complement marker
　长得　zhǎng de　(grow to) be —
　　(descriptive of physical
　　characteristics)

象　xiàng (SV) be alike
极了　-jíle (SV comp) extremely
比　bǐ (V) compare
　　(CV) compared with
以为　yǐwéi (V) think that, have the
　　idea that, assume (
　　wrongly)
双生　shuāngshēng (N) twins
　双生兄弟　shuāngshēng xiōngdì (N)
　　twin brothers
聪明　cōngming (SV) intelligent, bright
　　clever
可爱　kě'ài (SV) lovable, likable,
　　lovely
性情　xìngqing (N) nature, temperament
不同　bù-tóng (SV) dissimilar, differ-
　　ent

118

有(一)点儿 yǒu (yì)diǎnr (A) some-what, rather

慢 màn (SV) slow

性子 xìngzi (N) temper

连...也/都... lián ...yě/dōu... (CV) even (including)

比较 bǐjiào (V) compare
(A) comparatively, rather

急 jí (SV) impatient, anxious, hasty, urgent

不得了 bùdéliǎo (SV) terrible, disastrous
(SV comp) awfully, terribly

唱 chàng (V) sing

歌(儿) gē(r) (N) song
唱歌(儿) chàng-gē(r) (V-O) sing (a song)

整天 zhěngtiān (TW) all day long

一块儿 yíkuàir (A) together (= yìqǐ)

形影不离 xíng-yǐng bù lí (set phrase) inseparable (as form and shadow)

-得多 -de duō (SV comp) (by) a lot; much — er

好奇 hàoqí (SV) curious, inquisitive

各 gè (AT) each, all, various, different
各种各样 gè zhǒng gè yàng all sorts of

有的 yǒude (SP) some (always used as AT)

道理 dàolǐ (N) reason, sense, principle
有道理 yǒu-dàolǐ (=SV) reason-able, justified

奇怪 qíguài (SV) strange, odd

回答 huídá (V/N) answer, reply

雨 yǔ (N) rain
下雨 xià-yǔ (V-O) to rain

窗户 chuānghu (N) window

差 chà (SV) poor, substandard

糊涂 hútu (SV) muddled, silly

大人 dàren (N) adult, grown-up

麻烦 máfan (SV) troublesome, annoying
(V) put sb. to trouble
(N) trouble, bother

记 jì (V) memorize, remember, record

部首 bùshǒu (N) radical (of a Chinese character)

比方 bǐfang (N) example
比方说 bǐfang shuō (IE) for example

三点水 sān diǎn shuǐ (N) 'water' radical

关系 guānxi (N) relation(ship), relevance
A 跟 B 有关系 A is connected with B

林 lín (BF) forest, woods (in compound words)

木 mù (BF) tree, wood (in compound words)

X 字旁 X-zìpáng (N) lateral radical X

树木 shùmù (N) trees

有意思 yǒu-yìsi (SV) interesting

明白 míngbai (SV) clear, plain, obvious
(V) understand

嘴 zuǐ (N) mouth

茶杯 chábēi (N) teacup

木头 mùtou (N) wood (the material)

杯子 bēizi (N) cup, glass

笨 bèn (SV) stupid, obtuse, clumsy

意思 yìsi (N) meaning; idea; inten-tion; opinion
对 X 有意思 have designs on X

才 cái (A) only, merely

白 bái (SV) white; fair, pale (of complexion)

没关系 méi guānxi (IE) it doesn't matter; never mind

119

PRESENTATION

住在我们三楼的老张夫妇有两个男孩子,大的八岁,小的六岁.兄弟俩都是苹果脸儿,大眼睛,长得象极了.虽然哥哥比弟弟高一点儿,弟弟比哥哥胖一点儿,可是还有不少人以为他们是双生兄弟.这两个孩子一样聪明,一样可爱,不过他们的性情完全不同.哥哥有点儿象父亲,是个慢性子:说话说得慢,走路走得慢,连吃饭也吃得慢.弟弟比较象母亲,是个急性子,做什么事都急得不得了:看书看得快,写字写得快,连跟小朋友一起唱歌儿也比别人唱得快.两兄弟从小就玩儿得很好,整天在一块儿,形影不离.哥哥虽然只比弟弟大两岁,可是知道的事情好象比弟弟多得多.弟弟非常好奇,各种各样的问题多极了.有的问得很有道理;有的奇怪得谁也没法子回答.那天外头雨下得很大,不能出去玩儿,哥哥坐在窗户旁边儿看书,弟弟一边儿写字,一边儿跟哥哥说话:

DIALOGUE

A:哥,你来看看我这几个字写得好不好.

B:你是怎么写的?!今天比昨天写得更差了.

A:为什么我的字总是这么难看呢?我真不想写了!

B:写字不能太快,你写得太快了.

A:可是爸爸比我写得快得多,为什么写得那么好?

B:你真糊涂!爸是大人,小孩儿怎么能跟大人比?!

A:哥,中国字真麻烦,我记得快,忘得也快,你有什么好法子吗?

B:我们老师说学一个字应该先记这个字的部首,比方说'湖'这个字有三点水儿,一定跟水有关系,'林'这个字是'木'字旁儿,一定跟树木有关系.

A:这真有意思,现在我才明白为什么'吃'跟'喝'都是'口'字旁儿.

B:当然了,要是没有嘴,怎么吃,怎么喝啊?

A:可是茶杯的'杯'字儿为什么是'木'字旁儿呢?我从来没见过木头做的杯子.

B:你真笨,怎么连这个都不懂!你看'杯'这个字,一边儿是'木',一边儿是'不',意思就是说杯子不是木头做的!

120

SKETCHES

(1)

A：你的汉语说得真漂亮！

B：说得不好,我不会说.

A：你在这儿学了几年了？

B：我才学了四个月.

A：四个月就说得这么流利,真不容易!你们一个星期学几课？

B：我们学得非常快,有的时候学两课,有的时候学三课.

A：这是你写的汉字吧？写得真好.

B：难看极了,您别看了.

A：你们那位老师教得怎么样？

B：教得好极了,每一个字,每一句话,都解释得很清楚.

A：我跟你们老师住得很近,常常见面,你知道吗？

B：当然知道,要是不知道我就不这么说了.

(2)

A：李家两姐妹,姐姐比妹妹大几岁？

B：只大一岁半.

A：是不是姐姐书念得比妹妹好？

B：不错,妹妹虽然比姐姐聪明一点儿,可是姐姐比妹妹用功得多.

A：姐妹俩谁比较漂亮？

B：这就很难说了.两个人长得都很好看,姐姐比妹妹高一点儿,妹妹比姐姐白一点儿.

A：两个人谁比谁能干？

B：都很能干.姐姐做家里的事比妹妹做得快,妹妹出去办事比姐姐办得好.

A：你比较喜欢谁？

B：我喜欢谁都没用,因为他们姐妹俩都不喜欢我.

A：噢!真对不起,我以为.....

B：没关系,我本来对他们也没意思!

SPEECH PATTERNS

(1) Predicative complements

Patterns:　a.　　V _de_ 　SV (_bu_ SV)　　　V _de_ A　SV
他说得 流(利) 不流利？ 他说得不太流利.

b.　　V O 　V _de_ (A) SV
他说汉语说得 很流利.

or　　　O 　V _de_ (A) SV
他汉语说得 很流利.

1. 今天他来得早不早？ 　很早,七点钟就来了.

2. 他吃饭吃得很慢吗？ 　他吃饭吃得不慢,做事做得很慢.

3. 你什么地方不舒服吗？
没有不舒服,不过这两天晚上睡得不太好.

4. 昨天你不在家吗？
我带孩子上公园儿去了,在那儿玩得很高兴.

5. 你好象精神不大好. 　最近太忙了,休息得不够.

6. 这个问题他解释得清不清楚？ 　他解释得非常清楚.

7. 你歌儿唱得怎么样？ 　对不起,我什么歌儿都不会唱.

8. 他开车开得好不好？ 　开得不错,就是开得比较快没人敢坐.

9. 第十二课的录音你们听了吗？
听了,录得很不好,一会儿慢,一会儿快.

10. 她中国菜做得怎么样？ 　她做得又快又好.

11a. 他买的那些东西都很贵. 　b. 他买得贵.

12a. 他说的没人懂. 　b.他说得很明白.

(2) Intensifying complements

Patterns:　a.　　　SV _de hěn_
天气冷得很.

b.　　　SV _jíle_
天气冷极了.

c.　　　SV _de bùdéliǎo_
天气冷得不得了.

d.　　　SV _de_ 　Clause
天气冷得谁都不想出去.

1. 他运气好得很,刚到车站,车就来了。
2. 这个人的性情(奇)怪得很,他从来不跟人说话。
3. 昨天我看的那个电影儿有意思极了。
4. 她中国话说得流利极了。
5. 你们星期六在老王家玩儿得怎么样?
   我们玩儿得高兴极了。
6. 外头冷得不得了,里头热得不得了,哪儿都不舒服。
7. 她说做这个菜最少得三天,麻烦得不得了。
8. 这个人糊涂得不得了,你跟他说什么,他都说'有道理,有道理'。
9. 今天整整忙了一天,我现在累得什么都不想做了。
10. 那个小女孩儿,大眼睛小嘴儿,漂亮得人见人爱。
11. 两天没吃饭,他饿得不能再走了。
12. 昨天雨大得我们没法子出去。

(3) Comparison

Patterns: a. A (neg) bǐ B SV   (ma?)
               他 (不) 比 我 慢。
          b. A V O V de (neg) bǐ B SV
               他 写 字 写 得 (不) 比 我 慢。
    or A V O (neg) bǐ B V de SV
               他 写 字 (不) 比 我 写 得 慢。
    or A O V de (neg) bǐ B SV
               他 字 写 得 (不) 比 我 慢。

1. 汉语比英语难吧?   差不多,都不容易。
2. 他是不是比你又高又胖?   他比我高,可是不比我胖。
3. 这两所儿房子,哪所儿好?
   很难说:这所儿比那所儿大,那所儿比这所儿漂亮。
4. 他们夫妇俩,谁的性情好?   先生的性情比太太好。
5. 这件事谁去办比较好?   你去比他去好。
6. 他跑得比你快吗?   他跑得比谁都快。/他比谁都跑得快。
7. 弟弟比哥哥聪明吗?   聪明,弟弟学得比哥哥又快又好。
8. 你怎么总是比别人累?   我睡得比他们都少。

9. 你牌打得不错吧？　　我不怎么会打,他们打得都比我好.

10. 他信写得好不好？　　写得有意思极了,写得比我们都好.

11. 这个问题她们俩都回答了吗？

　　都回答了,姐姐回答得比妹妹清楚.

12. 你们为什么比别人卖得贵？　　我们的东西比别人好.

(4) Comparison with 'gèng' and 'hái'

Pattern:　　　　　　A　bǐ　B gèng/hái　SV

　　　　他很高,可是他弟弟比他　更　　高.

1. 你比我聪明,可是他比你更聪明.

2. 你说得不错,不过他比你更有道理.

3. 说中国话已经够麻烦了,写汉字比说中国话更麻烦.

4. 王大夫是不是伦敦最有名的大夫？

　　不是,李大夫比他更有名.

5. 他比你忘得快,可是我比他忘得更快.

6. 她又聪明又用功,中国话说得比中国人还好.

7. 他弟弟骑车骑得比汽车还快.

8. 这个字他学了三百次了还不认识,真是比牛还笨!

(5) Degrees of comparison

Patterns:　a.　A　bǐ　B　SV　yìdiǎnr
　　　　　　他　比　我　胖　一点儿.
　　　　　b.　A　bǐ　B　SV　de duō
　　　　　　他　比　我　胖　得多
　　　　　c.　A　bǐ　B　SV　duōle
　　　　　　他　比　我　胖　多了.
　　　　　d.　A　bǐ　B　SV　NU M
　　　　　　他　比　我　胖　八公斤.

1. 你说住楼上好,还是住楼下好？

　　大概住楼上(比住楼下)好一点儿.

2. 前头的窗户大,还是后头的窗户大？

　　前头的(比后头的)大一点儿.

124

3. 你们俩的英文谁说得流利？　她(说得)比我流利得多.

4. 你比他聪明吧？　不不不,我比他笨得多.

5. 今天是不是比昨天冷点儿？　今天比昨天冷多了!

6. 他写得比从前好吗？　比从前差多了,不能比.

7. 你比你妹妹大几岁？　只大一岁三个月.

8. 你的表快不快？　不快,比学校的钟慢两分.

9. 这种比那种贵多少？　贵一块半.

10. 他的钱比你多多少？　一个月多十二块.

11. 她教书教得比你久吧？　对了,她教得比我久一点儿.

12. 你弟弟比你长得高吧？　他高多了,比我整整高一个头.

13. 他还是跑得很慢吗？
　最近他天天练跑,比以前跑得快多了.

14. 她解释得清不清楚？　很清楚,比老师解释得清楚得多.

(6) **Lián ... yě/dōu ...** construction

Patterns: a. **Lián** S **yě/dōu** V O
　　　　连　他　　都　　知道这件事.
　　　 b. S **lián** O **yě/dōu** V
　　　　他　连这件事　都　　知道.

1. 今天忙极了,我连午饭都没时间吃.
2. 他聪明得不得了,连电脑都比他慢.
3. 这个问题太简单了,连三岁的小孩儿都知道怎么回答.
4. 他会说几句中国话,可是连半个汉字都不认识.
5. 我今天连一分钱都没带,怎么能下馆子？
6. 你上楼找谁？楼上连一个人都没有.
7. 你怎么笨得连北京在哪儿都不知道?!
8. 他糊涂得连自己姓什么都忘了.
9. 我们高兴得连课也不想上了.
10. 她急得连饭都没吃就走了.
11. 他们玩儿得连时间都忘了.
12. 他唱得连东南西北都不知道了.

125

(7) 'Yìdiǎnr' and 'yǒu yìdiǎnr' contrasted

Patterns: a.　A　(bǐ B)　SV (yì)diǎnr　　(Comparison)
　　　　　　这个 (比那个) 大 (一) 点儿 .

　　　　 b.　A　yǒu (yì)diǎnr SV　　(Adverb)
　　　　　　这个 有 (一) 点儿 大 .

1a. 今天 (比昨天) 冷一点儿.

 b. 今天有点儿冷.

2a. 他的性情 (比他爱人) 急一点儿.

 b. 他人不错,可是性情有点儿急.

3a. 这件事 (比那件事／比别的事) 麻烦点儿.

 b. 这件事有点儿麻烦.

4a. 要是他 (比现在) 高一点儿,就更象他哥哥了.

 b. 他长得有点儿象他哥哥.

5. 孩子们都有点儿好奇,所以常常问大人没法子回答的问题.

6. 这个人有点儿糊涂,连自己家多少号都不知道.
　　(Contrast: 这个人比较聪明.)

7. 我觉得这课有点儿难.
　　(Contrast: 他觉得这课很容易.)

8. 他说的那个办法有点儿奇怪.
　　(Contrast: 她说的那个办法很有道理.)

9. 你说别人都比他用功,他好象有点儿不高兴.
　　(Contrast: 她今天好象很高兴.)

10. 他今天有点儿不舒服,不能来上课.
　　(Contrast: 她今天精神好得很.)

接	jiē (V) to join; to receive (mail); to meet (welcome) sb.; to answer the phone	搬	bān (V) to move
封	fēng (V) to seal (M) for letters 信封 (N) envelope	乡	xiāng [鄉] * countryside; rural
邮	yóu [郵] * postal (V) to post, to mail 邮票 postal stamp	和	hé (C) and (CV) with
贴	tiē [貼] (V) to stick (on), to paste	邻	lín * [鄰] neighbour 邻居; neighbouring; adjacent
龙	lóng [龍] (N) dragon (M:条) a surname	居	jū * to reside; to dwell; to be (in a certain position)
凤	fèng [鳳] (N) phoenix (M:只)	考	kǎo (V) to give/take an examination
舞	wǔ (N) dance * to dance	艺	yì * [藝] skill; art 文艺 literature and art
泼	pō [潑] (V) to sprinkle; to splash; to spill (SV) shrewish	术	shù * [術] skill; technique; method; tactics 美术 fine arts
力	lì * strength; power; force; ability	相	xiāng * each other; mutually
寄	jì (V) to send (by post) * to entrust	拿	ná (V) to take in the hand; to take hold of (CV) with
原	yuán * primary; original; former; unprocessed	入	rù (V) to enter; to join 入口 entrance
画	huà [畫] (V) to draw; to paint 画儿 (N) picture, painting	另	lìng (A) other; another; separately

世	shì * world 世界 (M) a generation/lifetime	旧	jiù　　　　　[舊] (SV) old (opp. of 新) (AT) second-hand; used; 　　　 former
界	jiè　　　　* boundary; realm; scope; circles (as 文艺界)	古	gǔ (SV) ancient, age-old
如	rú　　　　　* like, as; as if; such as 不如 not equal to; not as good as; inferior to	拉	lā (V) to pull; to draw; to play (a bowed instrument)
倒	dǎo (A) indeed; actually; as it happens (contrary to expec- tation)	帘	lián　　　*　[簾] hanging screen; curtain 帘子 窗帘 window curtains
许	xǔ　　　　　[許] (V) to permit, to allow 也许 perhaps; maybe a surname	阳	yáng　　　　　[陽] (N) the masculine or posi- tive principle in nature 太阳 the sun
预	yù　　　*　[預] in advance, beforehand	吹	chuī (V) to blow; to boast 吹牛; to play (wind instruments); to fall through (of plans)
备	bèi　　　*　[備] to prepare	灯	dēng　　　　[燈] (N) lamp; light
幅	fú (M) for pictures, paintings; 　　 width of cloth	实	shí　　　*　[實] solid; true; real; fact 实在 really, truly
特	tè　　　　* special(ly)	试	shì　　　　　[試] (V) to try; to test 考试 examination; test 口试 oral examination
街	jiē (N) street　　　　(M:条) 街道 streets (collective) 大街 main street	步	bù * on foot (M) a step; a move in a 　　 board game

接	扌 扩 护 护 接 接	入	丿 入
封	士 圭 封	另	口 号 另
邮	丶 冂 口 由 由 邮 邮	世	一 十 廿 廿 世
贴	丨 冂 贝 贝 贝 贴 贴	界	冂 田 田 界 界
龙	一 ナ 尢 龙 龙	如	く 女 女 如
凤	丿 几 凤 凤	倒	亻 佢 倒 倒
舞	无 丿 亠 二 仨 缶 舞 舞 舞	许	讠 订 订 许
	舛 丿 夕 夕 夕 夘 舛	预	丶 マ 孑 予 予 预 预
泼	氵 汃 沙 泼 泼 泼	备	丿 夕 久 各 备 备
力	フ 力	幅	丨 冂 巾 帆 幅 幅
寄	宀 宀 字 害 寄	特	丿 亠 牛 牛 牪 牪 特
原	一 厂 厂 厎 原	街	彳 彳 往 往 街 街
画	一 一 冂 向 画 画 画	旧	丨 旧
搬	扌 扩 扩 拘 拚 拚 搬 搬 搬	古	一 十 古 古
乡	乚 纟 乡	拉	扌 扩 拉 拉
和	丿 千 禾 和	帘	宀 宀 穷 帘
邻	人 人 今 令 邻	阳	阝 阝 阳
居	フ コ 尸 尸 屋 居	吹	口 叻 吹
考	一 十 土 耂 考 考	灯	丷 火 火 灯
艺	一 艹 艺	实	宀 宀 字 实 实
术	一 十 木 术	试	讠 订 订 试 试
相	木 相 相 相	步	丨 卜 止 止 牛 步
拿	人 合 合 盒 拿		

前天 qiántiān (TW) day before yesterday

接(到) jiē(dào) (V) receive

封 fēng (M) measure for letters (V) seal

邮票 yóupiào (N) postage stamp

贴 tiē (V) stick (on)

信封 xìnfēng (N) envelope

毛笔 máobǐ (N) brush (for writing)

龙飞凤舞 lóng-fēi fèng-wǔ (set phrase) 'dragon flies, phoenix dances': flamboyant

活泼 huópo (SV) lively, vivacious

有力 yǒu-lì (SV) forceful

当时 dāngshí (TW) then, at that time

寄 jì (V) send, post

当中 dāngzhōng (PW) among, in the middle

等到 děngdào (TW) by the time, when ('wait till')

打开 dǎkāi (V) open

发现 fāxiàn (V) discover

原来 yuánlái (MA) originally; as a matter of fact, actually

画家 huàjiā (N) painter

搬(到) bān(dào) (V) move (to)

乡下 xiāngxia (PW) country (as opposed to town)

和 hé (C/CV) and, with (similar to gēn 跟)

邻居 línjū (N) neighbour

画儿 huàr (N) painting, picture

念完 niànwán (V) finish studying

-完 -wán (V comp) finish —ing

画画儿 huà-huàr (V-O) to paint, to draw

考 kǎo (V) give/take an examination, test

考上 kǎoshàng — (V) pass exam for —

艺术 yìshù (N) art (SV) artistic

学院 xuéyuàn (N) college

相当 xiāngdāng (A) quite, considerably, pretty

专心 zhuānxīn (SV) single-minded, engrossed

只要 zhǐyào (MA) it only needs; if only; as long as ....

一...就... yī ... jiù ... once/as soon as ... then...

拿 ná (V) take in the hand, hold
拿起来 náqilai (V) pick up

进入 jìnrù (V) enter into

另外 lìngwài (A) besides, separately (AT) another

世界 shìjiè (N) world

面前 miànqián (PW) in front of, in face of

如果 rúguǒ (MA) if (= yàoshi 要是)

简直 jiǎnzhí (A) simply

睡不着 shuìbuzháo (V) unable to get to sleep

-着 -zháo (V comp) get to (indicates attainment of objective)

130

怪人　guàiren (N) strange person, eccentric

倒(是)　dào(shi) (A) indeed, actually, as it happens (marks something contrary to the general drift or line of thought)

谈得来　tándelái (V) able to talk to/get on with

本　běn (SP) this, the present

也许　yěxǔ (MA) perhaps

预备　yùbèi (V) prepare, make ready

叫门　jiào mén (VO) call at the door (to be let in)

说不定　shuōbudìng (V) can't say for sure
(MA) maybe

果然　guǒrán (MA) sure enough, just as predicted

大半天　dà bàntiān (TW) greater half of a day; 'ages'

幅　fú (M) for paintings; width (of cloth)

门外汉　ménwàihàn (N) layman

特别　tèbié (SV/A) special(ly), particular(ly)

叫好　jiào-hǎo (V-O) 'shout well-done'; applaud

街　jiē (N) street

旧　jiù (SV) old; second-hand; former

古　gǔ (SV) old, ancient

关　guān (V) close, shut up/in, turn off

　关上　guānshang (V) close to

拉　lā (V) pull

　拉上　lāshang (V) pull to

窗帘(儿)　chuānglián(r) (N) window curtains

见不得　jiànbudé (V) may not be seen by/ exposed to

太阳　tàiyáng (N) sun

吹　chuī (V) blow

　吹不得　chuībudé (V) may not be blown (by)

风　fēng (N) wind

开　kāi (V) open; turn on

灯　dēng (N) lamp, light

客气　kèqi (SV) polite; formal; modest in manner

　不(要)客气　(IE) don't mention it! please don't bother

实在　shízài (A) in reality, honestly, really

笔　bǐ (M) stroke (with a pen or brush)

老兄　lǎo xiōng (N) (form of address between male friends) 'old chap'

考试　kǎoshì (N/V) (have an) examination

进步　jìnbù (V/N/SV) progress; progressive

一般　yìbān (SV/A) general, common, ordinary; generally, equally (used before SV)

不好意思　bù-hǎoyìsi (IE) embarrassed, ill at ease

前天中午我忽然接到一封不知从哪儿来的信,连邮票也没贴.信封上的字是用毛笔写的,龙飞凤舞,活泼有力.当时我想不出这封信是谁寄给我的.因为我的朋友当中没有一个能写得了这么漂亮的毛笔字.等到打开信才发现原来是老高写来的.没想到两年不见,我这位画家朋友的字已经练得这么好了.老高搬到乡下去以前和我是邻居.他五岁开始学画儿,中学没念完就考上了艺术学院.现在已经相当有名了.他画画儿的时候非常专心,只要一拿起笔来就好象进入了另外一个世界.谁走过他面前,他也看不见;谁跟他说话,他也听不见.如果一张画儿没画完,他简直饭也吃不下,觉也睡不着.朋友们都说他是个怪人.我虽然不懂艺术,可是跟他倒很谈得来.他信上说本月十八号要进城,如果有时间,也许来看我.今天就是十八号,我已经预备好了饭菜,他怎么还不来呢?欸,你听,外头有人叫门,说不定就是老高……

DIALOGUE

A: 来了,来了,听见了!谁啊?

B: 我啊,猜得出我是谁吗?

A: 老高,果然是你!快进来,快进来,已经等你大半天了.吃过饭没有?

B: 怎么?一进门就要请我吃饭?别急,别急,请你先看看我带来的这幅画儿.

A: 你知道我对画儿完全是门外汉,什么也看不懂.

B: 这幅画儿很特别,我敢说你看完了一定叫好.今天运气真不错,没想到在东大街那家旧书店买到了这么一幅古画儿.

A: 噢!是刚买的,那么就请你快点儿拿出来吧.

B：不行,得先麻烦你关上窗户,拉上窗帘儿。

A：为什么?这幅画儿有什么见不得人的地方吗?

B：你看你想到哪儿去了!这幅古画儿已经有三百年了,不是见不得人,是见不得太阳,吹不得风,请你快开开灯吧!

A：这画的是竹子吗?我怎么看不清楚?老高啊,说句不客气的话,我实在不知道这幅画儿好在哪里。

B：你看,你看这一笔,就这一笔最少也得二十年的功夫。

A：二十年的功夫?! 对不起,我看不出来。

B：老兄啊,要想看得出来,恐怕也得二十年!

SKETCHES

(1)　A：哥,你在楼上吗?看见今天的报没有?

　　　B：在我这儿,我还没看完呢。

　　　A：你还要多久才能看完?先拿下来给我看看行不行?

　　　B：你想看报?! 你的练习做完了吗?

　　　A：吃饭以前就做完了。

　　　B：你不是说明天考试吗?都预备好了吗?

　　　A：早就预备好了。

　　　B：昨天那个数学问题还没搞清楚吧。

　　　A：搞清楚了。

　　　B：欸,刚才妈叫你上街去买鱼,买到了吗?

　　　A：已经买回来了。

　　　B：那...那么你想干吗?

　　　A：我不想干吗,只想看看今天的报。

(2) A: 你中文学得怎么样了?进步很快吧?

B: 不行,我学得比一般人都慢,简单的话虽然能听懂不少了,可是一开口,就常常说错,真不好意思!

A: 你别不好意思了,我们中国人说英文的时候错得更多.你这么用功一定可以学得好.

B: 不用功不行啊!你看我们一天就有这么多练习,我不睡觉也做不完.

A: 别着急,你已经学得不错了.我们去食堂吃饭吧.

B: 这些练习没做完,我什么也吃不下.

A: 不吃饭怎么能有精神学习呢?

B: 那就麻烦你替我买一块三明治好不好?

A: 一块三明治吃得饱吗?两块吧.

B: 不,一块就够了.你不知道,我一吃饱了就想睡觉,更没法子学了.

SPEECH PATTERNS

(1) Resultative complements

(a) Some common resultative complements

Complements	Stem verbs
-见 (sensory perception)	看,听,碰...
-到 (arrival, attainment)	看,找,走,买,寄,送,想,学...
-着 (attainment)	找,见,买,睡...
-完 (completion)	做,说,吃,写...
-好 (satisfaction, completion)	做,写,办,预备...
-会 (learning mastery)	学,搞...
-懂 (understanding)	看,听,搞...
-开 (detachment, separation)	开,打,拉...
-定 (definiteness)	说...
-住 (fixity, secureness)	拿,记,贴...
-对 (correctness)	做,说,写,搞...
-错 (error)	做,说,写,搞...

- 清楚 (clarity)　　　　　　说,写,看...

- 饱 (repleteness)　　　　　吃,喝...

(b) Use of resultative complements

> Pattern:　你接到我的信了吗?
> or　你接到我的信没有?　　接到了。/ 没接到。

1. 你看,山上有两个人。　　我早就看到了,好象是老张和小李。
2. 你听,外头有人叫你。　　是吗?我怎么没听见?你听错了吧!
3. 孩子们都上楼睡觉了吗?　　都上去了,已经睡着了。
4. 老王昨天做的鱼怎么样?　　听说好吃极了,我去晚了,没吃着。
5. 这本小说你快看完了吧?　　我才看了一半,也许明天可以看完。
6. 那张画儿你还没画好吧?　　画好了,不过画得非常不好。
7. 你们明天到乡下去,预备好了吗?
   差不多都预备好了,希望明天别下雨。
8. 你学过太极拳吗?　　学过,可是没学会。
9. 他写的字龙飞凤舞,很不容易看懂。
   容易看懂就不够艺术了。
10. 开门,开门,我回来了!　　门已经开开了,快进来吧!
11. 他这个字是不是写错了?
    你开开灯我看看,是没写对,这儿少了一笔。
12. 那个地方很好找,你只要记住在图书馆的东边儿就行了。
13. 刚才收音机上是不是说明天有大风?　　我没听清楚。
14. 我们已经说定了,谁先做完练习谁去买东西。
15. 我发现除了他以外,还有另外一个人也看到了这件事。

(2) Directional complements

(a) Some common directional complements

Complements	Stem verbs
— 上 (up; on; attainment)	关,拉,戴,考...

- 下　(down; having room for)　　　坐,吃...

- 来　(in this direction)　　　上,下,进,出,回,拿,送,带,寄,搬...

- 去　(in that direction)　　　(ditto)

- 进　(in, into)　　　搬,拿,带,跑,走...

- 出　(out)　　　(ditto)

- 到　(arrive)　　　走,跑,学,寄,搬,拿...

- 过　(pass)　　　走,吃,看...

- 走　(away)　　　拿,搬,带,送...

- 上来　(come up)　　　拿,搬,送,跑,走...

- 下来　(come down)　　　(ditto)

- 上去　(go up)　　　(ditto)

- 下去　(go down)　　　(ditto)

- 进来　(come in)　　　(ditto)

- 出来　(come out)　　　(ditto)

- 进去　(go in)　　　(ditto)

- 出去　(go out)　　　(ditto)

- 起来　(rise, get up)　　　想,拿...

(b) Use of directional complements

　　Patterns: a.　　　V　DC　O
　　　　　他 关 上 窗户, 拉 上 窗帘, 就 去 睡 觉 了.
　　　　　　b.　　　V　DC　O　　(lai/qu)
　　　　　他 拿 出 一 幅 画儿　来　请 大家 看.

1. 他 戴 上 表, 关 上 门, 就 出 去 了.
2. 坐 下, 坐 下, 有 话 坐 下 再 说.
3. 如果 你 没 时间 送 来, 寄 来 也 可以.
4. 你 弟弟 去年 考 大学 没有?　考 了, 可是 没 考 上.
5. 寄 到 中国 去 的 信 得 贴 多少 钱 的 邮票?
6. 我 以为 那 家 书店 还 在 老 地方, 原来 他们 已经 搬 到 另外 一 条 街 上 去 了.
7. 他 用功 得 不得了, 每天 晚上 都 要 念 到 一、两 点.

136

8. 你常碰见他吗?

   我们是邻居,常碰见,我每天都得走过他家门口两次.

9. 吃过饭了吗?　　吃过了,连咖啡都喝过了.

10. 你心里有什么话,请你都说出来吧!

11. 学生们正要跑出去玩儿的时候,老师从外边儿走进来了.

12. 原来住在那儿的人已经搬走了,我们打算下月三号搬进去.

13. 你看见他那幅古画儿了吗?

   他本来已经拿出来了,看见你来,又拿回去了.

14. 他说的话你们都写下来了吗?　　每个字都写下来了.

15. 她这封信的意思,你看出来了没有?

   我没看出来有什么特别的意思.

16. 我今天带的钱不够,得回家去再拿点儿来.

17. 我刚走进去,他就拿起一份报来叫我看.

18. 你不是已经睡觉了吗?怎么又跑下楼来了?

   我忽然想起一件事来...

(3) <u>Potential complements</u>

(a) Some common potential complements

Affirmative	Negative	
见得	见不得	can be seen; be obvious/cannot be presented to
吃得	吃不得	may/may not be eaten
听得见	听不见	can/cannot hear
找得到	找不到	can/cannot find
睡得着	睡不着	can/cannot get to sleep
做得完	做不完	can/cannot finish doing
学得好	学不好	can/cannot master
看得懂	看不懂	can/cannot make out, understand, read
记得住	记不住	can/cannot remember
办得了	办不了	can/cannot carry out
吃得饱	吃不饱	can/cannot eat one's fill

	说不定	cannot say for sure
谈得来	谈不来	can/cannot get along with
考得上	考不上	can/cannot pass the exam for
坐得下	坐不下	can/cannot sit down or seat
上得去	上不去	can/cannot go up
下得去	下不去	can/cannot go down
走得上去	走不上去	can/cannot walk up
吃得下去	吃不下去	can/cannot carry on eating <u>or</u> get food down
看得出来	看不出来	can/cannot detect
开得进去	开不进去	can/cannot drive in
对得起	对不起	not let/let (someone) down

(b) Use of potential complements

Patterns: a. 你看得懂中文吗?

b. 你看得懂看不懂中文?

看得懂./ 看不懂.

1. 你看房子上有两个人. 在哪儿啊? 我怎么看不见?

2. 练习做完了吗? 还没呢,这么多,恐怕今天做不完.

3. 中国人说话你能听得懂吗?

   如果说的是普通话,我也许能听得懂.

4. 这么热,快开开窗户吧! 我刚才开了半天,开不开.

5. 我想买一幅中国画儿,不知道在这儿买得着买不着.

6. 世界上的事情真奇怪,想吃饱的人吃不饱;可以吃饱的人不吃饱.

7. 这件事他一个人去,办得了办不了?

   他那么能干,一定办得了.

8. 这么难写的字,你记得住记不住? 不必问,当然记不住.

9. 我和老王从小就很谈得来,现在还是好朋友.

10. 今天星期天不上班,什么人也找不到.

11. 明天我们学得到第十五课吗? 说不定,也许学得到.

12. 如果明年你能考上大学…… 别'如果'了,我一定考不上.

13. 她这两天心里有事,饭也吃不下,觉也睡不着.

14. 这个地方坐得下一百个人吗?
坐不下,最多只能坐下三十个人.

15. 他们住在八楼,你走得上去吗?　我这么胖,恐怕走不上去.

16. 三明治太难吃了,我简直吃不下去.

17. 你看得出来这是谁写的字吗?　噢!我没看出这是字来.

18. 大门太小,汽车开不进去怎么办?　我也想不出什么办法来.

19. 你的画儿能不能拿出来给我们看看?
不行,不行,我的画儿实在见不得人.

20. 您别客气,再吃一点儿吧!
谢谢您,我不会客气,我真的吃饱了,实在吃不下了.

(4) Complement 'guò' and suffix '-guo' contrasted

1a. 你吃过饭了吗?
 b. 你吃过中国饭吗?

2a. 今天送信的来过了吗?　来过了,没有你的信.
 b. 他来过英国吗?　来过,一九七八年来过一次.

3a. 你已经走过了西门大街,你看后头那条就是.
 b. 你以前走过西门大街吗?　没有,这是第一次.

4a. 桌子上的菜每样你都吃过了吗?　除了鱼以外,我都吃过了.
 b. 桌子上的菜每样你都吃过吗?　有的吃过,有的没吃过.

5a. 这份中文报我已经看过了,你拿去看吧.
 b. 你看过中文报吗?　看过一次,看不懂.

(5) Predicative complements and potential complements contrasted

1a. 他做得好不好?　大家都说他做得好.
 b. 他做得好做不好?　他很专心,一定做得好.

2a. 她说得清(楚)不清楚?　她说得(相当)清楚.
 b. 她说得清楚说不清楚?　这么简单的问题,她说得清楚.

3a. 你比你哥哥跑得快吗？　　我比他跑得快。

b. 你跑得快跑不快？　　如果前头有好吃的东西,我当然跑得快。

4a. 这个字他写得不对。

b. 这个字他写了十次了,可是还是写不对。

5a. 他喝得不多,只喝了一杯。

b. 他喝不多,一杯就够了。

(6) 'Gei' used as a verb complement

Pattern:　　　Vgei　Ind O　Dir O
　　　　　　　他寄给　　我一本书。

1. 快吃吧,这是妈特别做给你吃的。

2. 这是他的毛衣,昨天忘在这儿了,麻烦您带给他好吗？

3. 你那封信是写给谁的？

4. 那件事你能不能说给我们听听？　　恐怕我说三天也说不完。

5. 我不知道你要买旧车,我已经卖给别人了。

6. 他的那幅中国画儿已经送给大学图书馆了。

7. 报上的字太小,我看不清楚,请你念给我听听。

8. 她想看看我刚买的那本旧书,请你拿给她。

9. 他借给我的那本小说没什么意思,写得很一般。

10. 听说你认识那位张小姐,能不能介绍给我弟弟？

(7) Coverb 'gei' and complement 'gei' contrasted

1a. 那本书我上星期就寄给他了,为什么他还没接到？

b. 那本书我上星期就给他寄去了,为什么他还没接到？ (= a)

c. 那本书我上星期就给他寄了,为什么那个人还没接到？ (=替他)

2a. 那辆车你卖给他了吗？

b. 那辆车你给他卖了吗？ (= 替他)

140

3a. 这是他写给我的另外一封信.
 b. 这是他给我写的另外一封信. (1. = a; 2. = 他替我写的.)

4a. 这份儿是他的,请你拿给他.
 b. 他没来,请你给他拿一份儿. (= 替他)

5a. 这本书借给我看看,行不行?
 b. 请你给我借本书看看,行不行? (= 替我)

(8) 'YI ... jiù ...'

1. 两点钟一到,老师就进来了.
2. 老师一进来,我们就都站起来了.
3. 我们一站起来,老师就说:"请坐,请坐!"
4. 老师一说'请坐',我们就都坐下了.
5. 我们一坐下,老师就开始说中国话了.
6. 老师一开始说中国话,我们就糊涂了.
7. 我们一糊涂,老师就不高兴了.
8. 老师一不高兴,就不想教了.
9. 老师一不想教,我们就学不好了.

10. 他一看见中国字就想睡觉.
11. 我一看见中国人就说不出话来了.
12. 她一吃中国菜就觉得不舒服.
13. 他一有钱就想上酒馆儿.
14. 他一喝酒就要说外国话.
15. 他爱人一听见他说外国话就想打他.

研	yán　　　　[研] (V) to grind fine * to study, to research	切	qiē (V) to cut, to carve, to 　　slice
究	jiū　　　　　* to investigate; after all 研究 (V/N) study, research	红	hóng　　　　[紅] (SV) red; revolutionary (N) bonus, dividend
越	yuè　　　　　* to pass over; to exceed 越...越...　　the more ... the more ...	烧	shāo　　　　[燒] (V) to burn; to roast; to 　　stew in soy sauce
受	shòu (V) to receive; to accept; 　　to suffer, to endure	肉	ròu (N) meat; flesh; pulp (of 　　fruit)
迎	yíng　　　　* to meet, greet, welcome	烤	kǎo (V) to roast; to bake; to 　　heat by the fire
但	dàn (C) but, yet (A) merely, only	鸭	yā　　　　*　　[鴨] duck 鸭子　　　　(M:只) 烤鸭 roast duck
黄	huáng　　　　[黃] (SV) yellow a surname	炒	chǎo (V) to sauté, to stir-fry
餐	cān * to eat; food; meal (M) for meals	豆	dòu　　　　* beans, peas 豆子
论	lùn　　　　[論] * to discuss; theory (CV) by (in units of) 不论 no matter, regardless	腐	fǔ　　　　* rotten, decay 豆腐 bean curd
地	de (K) adverbial marker	嫩	nèn (SV) tender; delicate (of 　　skin)
把	bǎ (V) to hold; to guard (CV) governing object dis- posed of before verb	香	xiāng (SV) fragrant, aromatic; 　　smell good (of food) (N) incense, incense sticks
当	dàng　　　　[當] (V) to regard as, to treat 　　as; to think (mistakenly) 　　that	花	huā (N) flower (SV) flowery, fancy, coloured (V) to spend (money, time)

成	chéng (V) to accomplish; to become; to change into (SV) all right, be OK	酱	jiàng [醬] (N) thick sauce; jam
谱	pǔ [譜] (N) list, chart; manual; score (of music)	油	yóu (N) oil, fat, grease, petrol (SV) oily; glib 酱油 soy sauce
万	wàn [萬] (NU) ten thousand 一万五(千)15,000 a surname	素	sù (SV) simple, plain * vegetarian food 素菜 吃素 to be a vegetarian
厨	chú * [廚] kitchen 厨房	奶	nǎi (N) milk; breast 牛奶 cow's milk
阵	zhèn [陣] (M) short period; spell of (N) formation of troops	盘	pán [盤] (N) tray; plate, dish (V) to coil up (M) game of chess, go, etc.
拼	pīn [拼] (V) to piece together; to spell (words) 拼音 Pinyin	米	mǐ (N) rice (hulled uncooked) * grain (M) metre
手	shǒu (N) hand (M:只,双) 好手 good hand, expert (M:把) 第一把手 number one man	筷	kuài chopsticks 筷子 (M:支,双)
锅	guō [鍋] (N) pot, pan, wok	刀	dāo (N) knife, one-edged sword (M:把) (M) slash (with a knife)
糖	táng (N) sugar; sweets	叉	chā * fork 叉子 (M:把); cross (mark) (V) to fork

醋	cù
	(N) vinegar; jealousy
	吃醋 (VO) feel jealous
		敬	jìng
			(V) to respect; to offer (
			    wine, tea, etc. to a
			    guest)

辣	là (SV) hot (of spices), pep- pery; ruthless	干	gān [乾] (SV) dry 干杯 drink a toast; bottoms up, cheers
咸	xián [鹹] (SV) salty * salted	务	wù [務] * affair; business (LC) be engaged in; must, be sure to
淡	dàn (SV) weak, insipid; light (in colour)	甜	tián (SV) sweet

酸	suān (SV) sour; sore, ache (N) acid	面	miàn　　　[麵] (N) flour; noodles 面条儿 炒面 chow mein
照	zhào (V) to shine on; look at one-self (as in a mirror) (CV) according to, following	盐	yán　　　[鹽] (N) salt

STROKE—ORDER

研	厂 石 石 矸 研 研
究	宀 宀 究 究 究
越	土 丰 走 走 起 起 越 越 越
受	' ′ ∽ ∽ ∽ 罒 叉 受
迎	′ ㇉ 卬 卬 迎
但	亻 但 但
黄	一 卄 共 莕 苦 荢 苗 黄
餐	叔 ' ㇏ ㇏ ㇏ ㇏ ㇉ 叔
	食 人 今 今 合 食 食
论	讠 讠 讥 论 论
把	扌 扣 扣 押 把
当	丨 ⺊ ⺊ ⺗ 当 当
切	一 士 切 切
红	乙 纟 纟 纟 红 红
烧	⺰ 火 灯 灶 炞 烧 烧
肉	丨 门 内 内 肉
烤	火 灶 炒 烤 烤
鸭	口 口 日 甲 鸭 鸭 鸭 鸭
炒	火 灯 灼 炒 炒
豆	一 石 亘 豆
腐	' 一 广 庐 府 府 腐 腐
嫩	女 女 妒 姤 嫩 嫩 嫩 嫩

香	' 二 干 千 禾 香
花	艹 艹 花 花
成	一 厂 万 成 成 成
谱	讠 讠 讠 谐 谐 谐 谱
万	一 丁 万
厨	一 厂 后 厍 厨
阵	阝 阝 阝 阵 阵 阵
拼	扌 扩 拌 拼 拼
手	' ㇈ 三 手
锅	丿 丿 钅 钅 钊 铝 锅
糖	丷 丷 半 米 籿 糖 糖 糖 糖
醋	丆 两 两 酉 酌 醋 醋
辣	一 亠 立 辛 辢 辢 辣 辣
咸	一 厂 厂 咸 咸 咸 咸
淡	氵 氵 氵 氵 淡 淡 淡
酱	丬 丬 丬 丬 丬 丬 酱 酱 酱
油	氵 氵 汩 油 油
素	二 丰 主 圭 素 素
奶	女 奶 奶
盘	' 亻 冎 舟 舟 舟 盘
米	丷 丷 半 米 米
筷	丿 ⺮ ⺮ 竹 竹 竺 笭 笓 筷

144

刀　丁刀

叉　フ又叉

敬　艹艹芍苟敬敬敬

干　一二干

务　ノク夂务务

甜　二十舌舌甛甜甜甜

酸　丆丙丙酉酽酸酸

照　日明照照

面　一丆丙而面面

盐　土圵圤盐盐盐

VOCABULARY

闻名　wénmíng (SV) renowned (N.B. of restricted use)

世界闻名　shìjiè wénmíng world-famous

研究　yánjiū (V/N) research, study, investigate

越...越...　yuè ... yuè ... (C) the more ... the more...

越来越...　yuè lai yuè ... (A) more and more ...

受欢迎　shòu-huānyíng (SV) be popular (receive welcome)

但是　dànshi (C) but, yet

黄　huáng (SV) yellow (a surname)

化学　huàxué (N) chemistry

专家　zhuānjiā (N) expert

思想　sīxiǎng (N) thought, thinking

看法　kànfǎ (N) outlook, view

西化　xīhuà (V/SV) Westernize(d)

-化　-huà (suffix) -ize, -ify

西餐　xīcān (N) Western food

餐　cān (BF) food, meal, cuisine (M) for meals

吃不来　chībulái (V) unable to take to (foods)

-来　-lái (V comp) (potential complement) able to, manage to

不论　búlùn (MA) no matter how, regardless

多(么)　duō(me), duó(me) (A) how, to what extent

好好儿(地)　hǎohāor(de) (A) properly, thoroughly

-地　-de (K) adverbial marker

要不然　yàoburán (C) otherwise

把　bǎ (CV) governing object disposed of before verb (M) for chairs, knives, etc.

当(做)　dàng(zuò) (V) treat as, regard as

白切鸡　báiqiējī (N) white/plain cut chicken

红烧肉　hóngshāoròu (N) red-cooked (pork) meat

烤鸭　kǎoyā (N) roast duck

点心　diǎnxin (N) various pastries and snacks

牛肉　niúròu (N) beef

炒　chǎo (V) stir-fry

豆腐　dòufu (N) bean curd

嫩　nèn (SV) tender, soft

烧　shāo (V) burn; cook, stew, bake

香　xiāng (SV) fragrant (N) incense

难得　nán-dé (SV) hard to get, rare

来历　láilì (N) history, antecedents, origin

为了　wèile (CV) for (the sake of), in order to

花　huā (V) spend (time, money)

工夫　gōngfu (N) time and effort; leisure time

心得 xīndé (N) knowledge gained

有条有理地 yǒu-tiáo-yǒu-lǐde (A) methodically, systematically

写成 xiěchéng (V) compile (fashion through writing)

-成 -chéng (V comp) so as to be, become

食谱 shípǔ (N) cookery book

万 wàn (NU) ten thousand

打进 dǎjìn (V) breach, invade

厨房 chúfáng (N) kitchen

意外(地) yìwài(de) (A) in an unforeseen manner

阵 zhèn (M) wave, spate, burst, spell

出风头 chū fēngtou (VO) create a stir, enjoy the limelight

大衣 dàyī (N) overcoat

拼起来 pīnqilai (V) put together

菜单 càidān (N) menu

点(菜) diǎn (cài) (VO) choose, order (dishes on menu)

拿手 náshǒu (SV) expert in, good at

拿手菜 náshǒu cài (N) speciality (dish)

家乡鸡 jiāxiāngjī (N) 'home town chicken'

回锅肉 huíguōròu (N) 'return to the pot meat' — twice-cooked pork

黄鱼 huángyú (N) yellow croaker (fish)

来 lái (V) bring (esp. food)

糖醋 tángcù (AT) sweet-and-sour (lit: sugar-vinegar)

辣 là (SV) hot (spices)

咸 xián (SV) salty, savoury

淡 dàn (SV) bland, mild

放 fàng (V) put; put in; let go

酱油 jiàngyóu (N) soy sauce

记得 jìde (V) remember, recall

素菜 sùcài (N) vegetable dish

奶油菜花 nǎiyóu càihuā (N) creamed cauliflower

奶油 nǎiyóu (N) cream

拼盘(儿) pīnpán(r) (N) cold platter

白菜牛肉汤 báicài niúròu tāng (N) cabbage and beef soup

米饭 mǐfàn (N) cooked rice

筷子 kuàizi (N) chopsticks

刀叉 dāo-chā (N) knife and fork

敬 jìng (V) salute, toast

干杯 gān-bēi (IE) drain glass, Cheers!

服务 fúwù (V/N) serve; service
服务员 fúwùyuán (N) attendant

甜 tián (SV) sweet

酸 suān (SV) sour

新手 xīnshǒu (N) new hand, novice

照 zhào (CV) according to, in conformity with

不当一回事 bú dàng yì huí shì (IE) not regard as a matter (of any importance)

锅贴儿 guōtiēr (N) fried dumpling

面 miàn (N) noodles

公事 gōngshì (N) official business; paperwork

盐 yán (N) salt

牛奶 niúnǎi (N) (cow) milk

糖 táng (N) sugar; sweets

哪里 nǎlǐ (IE) Not at all (often reduplicated) = nǎr de huà 哪儿的话

146

PRESENTATION

中国菜是世界闻名的,因为中国人研究吃的艺术已经有很长的历史了。最近一、二十年中国菜在英国越来越受欢迎,中国饭馆儿也越来越多。虽然这些馆子的菜都不错,但是很少有我朋友黄英白做得那么好的。老黄是位化学专家,来英国快四十年了,虽然思想和看法都已经相当西化,可是西餐还是吃不来的。每天不论多忙,他也要好好儿地做两个菜,舒舒服服地吃顿中国饭,要不然晚上连觉都睡不好。他把做菜当做一种艺术来研究:从白切鸡到红烧肉,从北京烤鸭到广东点心,他怎么做怎么好吃。他能把牛肉炒得跟豆腐一样嫩,也能把豆腐烧得象鱼一样香。更难得的是还能把每个菜的来历清清楚楚地说出来。为了把吃的艺术介绍给西方人,去年他花了五个月的工夫,把他多年的做菜心得有条有理地写成了一本食谱,没想到一个月就卖了两万本。中国菜打进了英国厨房,老黄也意外地出了一阵风头。有一天他请了几位朋友去吃中国馆子……

DIALOGUE

A: 您来了,几位啊?请这边儿坐。您把大衣都给我吧。

B: 我们一共六个人,有没有大一点儿的桌子?

A: 对不起,大桌子没有了。您早一点儿来就好了。这样吧,我把这两张小桌子给您拼起来怎么样?

B: 好吧,六个人坐得下就行。麻烦你先把菜单儿拿来给我们看看。

A: 好,马上就来。您都请坐,先喝杯茶。

B: 这菜单儿上的菜真不少,我越看越不知道点什么好,还是麻烦你介绍几样儿你们的拿手菜吧!

A: 我们这儿的家乡鸡、回锅肉是最拿手的.今天还有刚到的黄鱼,来个糖醋黄鱼怎么样?

B: 好啊,这三个菜都要,不过回锅肉不能太辣也不能太咸,做淡一点儿好吧?少放点儿酱油.欸,我记得你们这儿的红烧豆腐特别好吃,来个红烧豆腐,再要个素菜 —— 奶油菜花儿有吧?

A: 有有有.您几位喝不喝酒?要不要先来个拼盘儿?

B: 我们想喝点儿酒.好,先来个拼盘儿,最后再给我们来个白菜牛肉汤吧,我们都吃米饭.

A: 好,好.您这几位外国朋友是用筷子还是用刀叉?

B: 他们几位筷子用得比我还好,刀叉是用不着的.请你快点儿上菜吧.噢,还有,麻烦你把窗户关小点儿好吗?风太大了.

A: 拼盘儿来了!

B: 来来来,我先敬大家一杯.干杯啊!请请请,吃菜,吃菜,别客气,多吃点儿!

（服务员最后把汤拿上来以后,老黄问他:）

B: 奇怪啊,今天的糖醋鱼怎么又不甜又不酸?红烧豆腐也没有以前那么香了,你们厨房是不是换了新手?

A: 没有啊!不过我们厨房买了一本新出的食谱,今天的糖醋鱼和红烧豆腐完全是照那个食谱做的.听说写那本食谱的是位化学专家,叫黄什么曰.不知道您认不认.....

B: 不认识! 不认识! 不认识!

SKETCHES

(1) A: 欸,李大姐,什么风把你吹来了?真是难得!

B: 早就想来看你们,总是没工夫,你们都好吧?

A: 还那样儿.请坐,请坐!把大衣放在这儿吧.最近忙什么啊?

B: 我们厂预备把生产拉上去,大家都比以前忙多了.

A: 我们公司也没以前那么舒服了,为了要把服务搞得更好,一个人常常得做两个人的事.孩子们都好吧?

B: 现在都大了,整天往外跑,学习都很差.我真不知道你怎么能把孩子教得那么好.

A: 别说了,都一样.现在的孩子简直不把父母的话当一回事!欸,饿了吧,我请你去吃锅贴儿怎么样?

B: 你怎么把我当客人了,就在楼下食堂吃碗面不好吗?

A: 你这么久不来当然是客人了,能不能等我几分钟?我得先把这件公事拿给老王看看.

B: 没问题,你把应该办的事都办完,我多饿一会儿没关系,到了饭馆儿可以多吃一点儿.

(2) A: 您怎么吃这么少?请再多吃点儿菜!

B: 谢谢您,我真的吃饱了,已经比平常多吃了一碗饭.菜太好了!

A: 您太客气了,今天的菜做得都很差.我忙糊涂了,红烧鸡太咸,回锅肉太辣,汤里也忘了放盐.

B: 您别客气了,我觉得样样儿都好,特别是这个糖醋鱼,馆子里的都没这么好吃.

A: 要是再做甜一点儿就好了.....我们那边儿坐吧,您喝咖啡还是喝茶?

B: 给我一杯咖啡吧,我饭吃多了,酒也喝多了.

A: 您要不要牛奶?放几块糖?

B: 牛奶不要,您给我放两块糖吧.....这咖啡真香.....噢,已经十点一刻了,我得走了.

A: 您不多坐一会儿了吗?再喝杯咖啡吧.

B: 不了,我得早点儿回去,明天还要上班.谢谢您啊,今天真是把您累坏了.

A: 哪里,哪里.以后有工夫常来玩儿啊!您慢走,不送了.再见!

B: 再见!再见!请回!请回!

SPEECH PATTERNS

(1) The 'bǎ' construction

Pattern:　S　A (neg)　bǎ　O　V + other element
　　　　　　他　　　　把我的笔拿　走了.

1. 谁把我的茶喝了?
2. 今天太忙了,我把这件事忘了,真对不起.
3. 请你们先把这个问题研究研究,不必马上做决定.
4. 你能不能把这次去中国的经过跟我们谈谈?
5. 他们把麻烦都给我了,我把麻烦给谁呢?
6. 你可不可以把你教英文的心得告诉我?
7. 别把笔放在嘴里,快拿出来!
8. 他想把那一万本旧书送给图书馆.
9. 我已经把筷子,碗都拿到厨房去了.
10. 我们要搞'四化',不是要搞'西化',你怎么把'四'字看成'西'字了?
11. 她真能干,只花了半个小时的工夫就把十个人的饭菜预备好了.
12. 麻烦你拿刀把这块肉替我切切. (切 , 'to cut')
13. 我没把他当老师,他也没把我当学生.
14. 他把菜做得太咸了,我们一边儿吃,一边儿喝水.
15. 请你把这个字的用法再给我们解释一次.
16. 一会儿这样,一会儿那样,这个'把'字简直把我搞糊涂了.
17a. 这儿桌子太多,请你搬两张出去. (indefinite reference)
　b. 这儿桌子太多,请你把这两张搬出去. (definite reference)
18a. 这些字我们都写错了.
　b. 我们把这些字都写错了.
　c. 我们都把这些字写错了.
19a. 他把钱拿出来了. ～ 他拿出钱来了.
　b. 我已经把这句话的意思看懂了.～ 我已经看懂了这句话的意思.
　c. 他把研究历史的心得写成了一本书.
20a. 他吃什么了?　　他吃糖醋鱼了.
　b. 桌子上的菜他都吃了吗?　　糖醋鱼他吃了,红烧肉他没吃.
　c. 糖醋鱼呢?谁把糖醋鱼吃了?　　不是我.

150

(2) <u>Similarities</u>

(a) Equivalent or not

Patterns: a.　　A　　<u>gēn</u>　B　<u>yíyàng</u>/<u>bù yíyàng</u>

你 的 表 跟 我 的 一样.

b.　　A　　<u>gēn</u>/<u>xiàng</u>　　B　　<u>yíyàng</u> SV/MV+V

红烧肉　跟　　糖醋鱼 一样 好吃.

1. 中国画儿跟英国画儿很不一样.
2. '思想解放'跟'解放思想'完全一样吗?
3. 西餐的做法跟中餐不一样吧?
4. 今天的天气跟昨天一样好.
5. 这儿的风景象黄山一样漂亮.
6. 他跟我一样爱喝酒,我跟他一样喜欢吃辣的.
7. 你的看法跟他一样有道理.
8. 我们应该象他一样把中文学好.
9. 她菜做得跟她母亲一样有名.
10. 他普通话说得快象中国人一样流利了,进步真快.

(b) On a par with or not

Patterns: a.　　A　(<u>méi</u>)<u>yǒu</u>　B　<u>nàme</u>/<u>zhème</u> SV/MV+V

我 没 (有) 你 那么 聪明.

b.　　A　(<u>bú</u>) <u>xiàng</u>　B　<u>nàme</u>/<u>zhème</u> SV/MV+V

他 不 象 我 这么 笨.

1. 你弟弟有你这么高吗?　　我们俩差不多一般高.
2. 他的性情不象你这么急.
3. 她没有她妹妹那么活泼,也不象她姐姐那么爱出风头.
4. 他一定记得这件事,他没有我这么糊涂.
5. 谁敢说这儿的服务没有那儿好?
6. 中国人不象英国人这么喜欢喝牛奶.
7. 红烧肉没有烤鸭那么受欢迎.
8. 我菜没他炒得那么好,可是他肉切得没有我这么快.
9. 她九点半就睡了,不象我们睡得这么晚.
10. 他写汉字不象你这么龙飞凤舞.

(3) Situational 'de'

1. 北京我没去过,可是北京烤鸭我倒是吃过的.
2. 他从小吃米饭长大的,三明治是吃不来的.
3. 虽然他说话有点儿糊涂,可是办事还是有条有理的.
4. 他对化学也是非常有兴趣的.
5. 简单的菜我会炒两样,广东点心我是做不来的.
6. 他太喜欢这张画儿了,不论多贵,他也要买的.
7. 这个人不专心,不论做什么,他总是搞不好的.
8. 他已经快二十了,你把他当做小孩子是不行的.
9. 她来信希望我别去,可是我还是要去的.
10. 如果你不用功,中文是学不好的!

(4) Adverbials marked with 'de'

1. 他整天(地)站在街上,什么事也不做.
2. 她整天楼上楼下地跑累得不得了.
3. 小朋友很活泼地跑出来欢迎我们.
   (cf. 小朋友很活泼,跑出来欢迎我们.)
4. 她来晚了,很不好意思地跟老师说:"对不起....."
   (cf. 她知道老师说错了,可是不好意思跟老师说.)
5. 这件公事他大概地看了看,就说没问题.
   (cf. 这件公事他大概已经看过了,你拿走吧.)
6. 他很清楚地把这个人的来历都告诉我了.
7. 我们很简单地预备了两样菜,想请他来吃顿饭.
8. 听见外头有人说中国话,他好奇地走出去看了看.
9. 他非常客气地问我能不能把我的拿手菜教给他.
10. 一看见我手上的糖,孩子们都高兴地跑过来了.
11. 他买了一块新表,把旧的很便宜地卖给他朋友了.
12. 他看见我们,高兴地说:"欢迎,欢迎!请进,请进!"
    (cf. 他看见我们,高兴得说不出话来了.)

(5) Reduplicated stative verbs as adverbials

(a) Monosyllabic SVs

1. 为了这个问题我整整地忙了三天,还是没搞好.
2. 你得好好儿地学习,要不然考试考不好.
3. 请你快快儿地把这些锅贴儿拿回厨房去.
4. 搬家的事得慢慢儿地研究,着急也没用.
5. 你的字写得太难看了,以后要多多(地)练习.
6. 做这个菜酱油不能太多,少少儿地放一点儿就够了.
7. 她晚上想去看戏,早早儿地就把晚饭吃了.
8. 他新写的那本小说在英国很受欢迎,上个月他来伦敦,大大地出了一阵风头.
9. 你应该好好儿地想想是去还是不去.
10. 他冷冷地说了一句'专家也得好好儿地干!'就走了.
11. 他把公司的老人慢慢地都换成了他自己的人了.

(b) Disyllabic SVs

1. 吃过午饭,孩子们都高高兴兴地上公园儿玩儿去了.
2. 我昨天清清楚楚地听见他说,那件事是他干的.
3. 别炒菜了,简简单单地吃碗面就行了.
4. 今天晚上舒舒服服地睡一觉,明天就有精神了.
5. 大家客客气气地在一起工作,不好吗?
6. 希望你能有条有理地把这件事的经过写出来.
7. 你最好实实在在地告诉我们,你是来干吗的?
8. 这么冷的天气,谁不想舒舒服服地在家里休息?
9. 他信上明明白白地说要给我一万块钱,怎么还不寄来呢?
10. 我们应该实实在在地为人民服务!

(6) <u>Adverbials and predicative complements contrasted</u>

1a. 请你好好儿地写两个毛笔字.
  b. 你这两个毛笔字写得真好.

2a. 他慢慢儿地把事情都做完了.
  b. 他做事做得很慢.

3a. 那个收音机他们很便宜地卖给我了.
  b. 那个收音机他们卖得很便宜.

4a. 他们很高兴地在湖边儿玩儿了一下午.
  b. 那天下午他们在湖边儿玩儿得很高兴.

5a. 他清清楚楚地把这个问题解释了一次.
  b. 这个问题他解释得非常清楚.

(7) <u>Verb constructions that show comparative degree</u>

(a) Complements: V SV <u>yìdiǎnr</u>

1. 请你站近一点儿,看清楚一点儿那不是伦敦地图:
2. 对不起,您说得太快了,请您说慢一点儿好吗?
3. 你的字太小了,我看不清楚,请你写大一点儿.
4. 上课的时间快到了,走快一点儿吧. (我们走得不够快.)
5. 这张画得完全不象,请你画好一点儿.
6. 今天出去旅行,我们得吃饱一点儿.
7. 这么热,请你把窗户开大点儿.
8. 你做的菜都太淡了,下次能不能请你做咸一点儿.
9. 一个月不够,我希望能在中国住久一点儿.
10. 请你把这个东西放高点儿,找个孩子拿不到的地方.

(b) Adverbials: SV <u>yìdiǎnr</u> V (SVs being <u>kuài</u>, <u>màn</u>, <u>zǎo</u>, <u>wǎn</u>)

1. 要下雨了,快点儿跑吧! (a. 马上开始跑. b. = 跑快点儿吧.)
2. 你慢点儿给钱,先看看东西好不好.
3. 面已经冷了,快点儿吃吧. (a. 马上开始吃. b. = 吃快点儿吧.)

4. 快点儿出去看看谁来了.

5. 明天请你早一点儿来. （=来早一点儿.）

6. 我得先去医院看个朋友,晚一刻钟到,行不行?

7. 早点儿开始可以早点儿做完.

8. 照他的说法,还是晚点儿结婚好. （=结婚晚点儿好.）

(c) SV V <u>yìdiǎnr</u>/NU M N (SVs: <u>duō</u>, <u>shǎo</u>, <u>zǎo</u>, <u>wǎn</u>)

1. 没什么好菜,可是请您多吃点儿.

2. 四块钱是少一点儿,多给他一块吧.

3. 你还有那么多事没做完呢,少看点儿电视吧.

4. 我知道你有道理,不过还是请你少说两句.

5. 大夫说我应该多吃点儿素菜,少吃点儿肉.

6. 我太胖了,咖啡里得少放点儿糖. (or:少放一块糖.)

7. 我敬你,多喝点儿啊!你看,我已经干了三杯了,你还是那一杯.

8. 今天的牛肉我多炒了两分钟,不够嫩了.

9. 明天请你们早来五分钟,可以吗?

10. 我们的车晚到了一刻钟.

(8) <u>Correlative clause</u>

Patterns: a.   <u>yuè</u>...<u>yuè</u>...
       他 越 说 越 快,越 快 我 越 听 不 懂.
    b.   <u>yuè lai yuè</u> ...
       他 越 来 越 糊 涂 了.
    c. <u>búlùn</u> QW   <u>yě</u>/<u>dōu</u>/<u>háishi</u> ...
       不 论 多 冷,他   都   不 买 大 衣.

1. 中文越学越有意思,越有意思我就越想学.

2. 点菜真不容易,这个菜单我越看越糊涂.

3. 钱是越多越好,工作是越少越好.

4. 新手都一样,越怕搞错越容易错.

5. 房子越住越小,汽车越坐越大.

155

6. 东西越来越贵,工作越来越难找.
7. 电脑越来越进步,人的脑子也就越来越没用.
8. 风越来越大,街上的人也越来越少,我心里也就越来越着急.
9. 喝咖啡的人越来越多,喝茶的人越来越少.
10. 不论你多忙,今天也得把这件公事办完.
11. 不论你给他多少钱,他也不干这种事.
12. 不论他说得多好听,我还是不想跟他去.
13. 不论你喜不喜欢都得照他的法子办事.
14. 不论你是谁,晚上十点以后我是不见客人的.
15. 不论换什么人来教他,他也学不好.

(9) Causative verbs

1. 客人都到了,可以上菜了.
2. 今天馆子人多,上菜上得真慢.
3. 中国南方出米,所以南方人都吃米饭.
4. 他希望每年能出一本书.
5. 说话的人很多,可是出钱的人很少.
6. 给我们来四十个锅贴儿,一大碗酸辣汤.
7. 麻烦你,再来点儿茶!
8. 这么多人,我得下多少斤面啊? (下面, 'cook (lit. 'lower') noodles')

室	shì * room 办公室 office	摆	bǎi [擺] (V) to put, to place, to arrange, to display
着	zhe [着] (V suffix) indicating contin- ued state or action	绿	lǜ [綠] (SV) green
套	tào (N) sheath, case, cover (V) to sheathe, to cover with (M) set, suit, suite	灰	huī (N) ashes; dust (SV) grey
沙	shā (N) sand (SV) (of voice) hoarse 沙发 sofa, settee	缸	gāng (N) vat, jar, mug, bowl
立	lì * to be standing (V) to set up	发	fà * [髮] hair (on the human head)头发
排	pái (V) to arrange (in a row); to line up 排队 (M) row, line; platoon	镜	jìng * [鏡] mirror 镜子; lens 眼镜儿 eye-glasses

架	jià
	* frame; rack; shelf
	(M) for machines, aeroplanes,
	     etc.
		穿	chuān
			(V) to pierce through; to
			     pass through; to put on
			     (clothes, footwear)

墙	qiáng [牆] (N) wall (M:面,道)	贸	mào * [貿] to trade 贸易
挂	guà [掛] (V) to hang, to suspend; to ring off (M) a string (of things)	历	lì * [曆] calendar 月历 monthly calendar
远	yuǎn [遠] (SV) far, distant, remote	里	lǐ * lane, square (in place names) (M) 1 里 里 = ½ km 公里
颜	yán * [顏] face; countenance; colour a surname	渐	jiàn * [漸] gradual(ly), by degrees
色	sè * colour 颜色; look	黑	hēi (SV) black; dark

低	dī (SV) low (V) to let droop, to lower (the head)	喂	wéi, wèi (I) Hello! (in telephoning); Hey!
屋	wū * house; room 屋子 (M: 间)	雪	xuě (N) snow 下雪 to snow
隔	gé (V) to separate, partition (CV) at a distance from; after or at an interval of	度	dù * standard; measure; degree of intensity (M) degree; occasion
紧	jǐn [緊] (SV) tight, tense; strict; urgent; hard up	故	gù * old; deceased; cause (LC) therefore 故事 story
轻	qīng [輕] (SV) light; gentle 年轻 young	宫	gōng [宮] (N) palace; hall
枪	qiāng [槍] (N) spear; rifle; pistol (M: 支)	伟	wěi * [偉] big; great; heroic

匹	pǐ
	(M) for horses, mules; a
	    bolt of cloth
		系	xì [繫]
			(V) to tie, to fasten; to
			    relate to

切	qiè * be close to; be anxious to; be sure to 一切 all, every(thing)	帮	bāng [幫] (V) to help (N/M) clique, gang, group 四人帮 the Gang of Four
铃	líng [鈴] (N) small bell	处	chù [處] * place, locality (M) department: office
响	xiǎng [響] (V) to sound, to make a sound (SV) loud, noisy	设	shè [設] (V) to set up, to establish

赶	gǎn [趕]
	(V) to hurry; to catch up
	    with; to drive (a cart);
	    to drive away
		续	xù * [續]
			to continue; to extend
			手续 procedures, formal-
			ities

途	tú * way, road, route 长途 long-distance	费	fèi [費] * fee; expenses, charge (V) to spend (money or time) a surname
线	xiàn [線] (N) thread; wire; line	镑	bàng [鎊] (M) pound (sterling)

病	bìng (SV) to be ill 病了，有病 (N) illness, disease; defect		

<u>STROKE-ORDER</u>

室　宀 宀 宀 室

着　丷 兰 关 着 着 着

套　大 太 本 夲 叁 套

沙　氵 沙 沙

立　亠 立 立

排　扌 扌 扌 扌 扌 排

架　フ 力 加 架

墙　土 土 土 土 圹 墙 墙

挂　扌 扌 挂

远　二 テ 元 远

颜　彦　亠 立 立 产 彦

　　页　一 ア 百 页 页

色　ク 夕 夕 多 色

摆　扌 扌 扌 摆 摆

绿　纟 纟 纟 纟 纟 绿 绿 绿

灰　一 ナ 力 灰 灰

缸　𠂉 二 午 缶 缶 缸

发　乚 ㄅ 岁 发 发

镜　钅 钅 钅 镜

穿　宀 穴 穴 空 穿 穿

贸　ノ 𠃌 𠃌 卬 卬 贸 贸

历　一 厂 历 历

里　丶 冂 日 旦 甲 里

渐　氵 氵 氵 洋 淖 渐 渐 渐

黑　冂 四 回 四 甲 里 黑

低　亻 亻 亻 仾 低 低

屋　一 コ 尸 层 屋

隔　阝 隔 隔 隔

紧　丨 丨 収 坚 紧

轻　一 七 车 车 轧 轻 轻

枪　木 朩 枪 枪

匹　一 厂 兀 匹

切　一 七 切 切

铃　钅 钅 铃 铃

响　口 口 叫 响 响

赶　土 丰 走 赶 赶

途　人 亼 今 余 途

线　纟 纟 线 线 线

喂　口 口 口 口 喂 喂 喂

雪　一 二 千 币 雨 雪 雪 雪

度　亠 广 广 广 庐 庐 度 度

故　十 古 古 故 故

宫　宀 宫 宫

伟　亻 亻 伟 伟

系　一 玄 系

帮　三 丰 邦 邦 帮 帮

处　夕 夂 处 处

设　讠 讠 设 设

续　纟 纟' 纩 纩 纩 续 续 续
费　一 二 弓 弗 弗 费 费

锣　钅 钌 钌 钌 锣 锣 锣
病　一 广 广 疒 病 病 病

VOCABULARY

间　jiān (M) for rooms

办公室　bàngōngshì (N) office

-着　-zhe (V suffix) durative suffix

套　tào (M) set, suit, suite

沙发　shāfā (N) sofa; easy chair

立　lì (V) stand; set up, establish

排　pái (M) a row of
　　　 (V) form a row

书架　shūjià (N) bookshelf

面　miàn (N) face, surface, side
　　　 (M) for walls

墙　qiáng (N) wall

挂　guà (V) hang

好几　hǎo jǐ (A NU) a good few —

山水(画儿)　shānshuǐ(huàr) (N)
　　　 landscape (paintings)

离　lí (CV) separated from

远　yuǎn (SV) far, distant

办公桌　bàngōngzhuō (N) (office)
　　　 desk

颜色　yánsè (N) colour

电话　diànhuà (N) telephone

摆　bǎi (V) place, lay out, display

绿(色)　lǜ(se) (SV) green (coloured)

烟灰缸　yānhuīgāng (N) ashtray

头发　tóufa (N) hair (on head)

灰白　huībái (SV) grey-white

眼镜儿　yǎnjìngr (N) spectacles

穿　chuān (V) wear, put on (of
　　　 garments)

西服　xīfú (N) Western clothes; suit

中年人　zhōngnián rén (N) middle-aged
　　　 person

贸易　màoyì (N) trade

总经理　zǒngjīnglǐ (N) general mana-
　　　 ger

总　zǒng (AT) general, chief, head;
　　　 overall

对面　duìmian (PW) opposite

月历　yuèlì (N) monthly calendar

在　zài (CV) engaged in, in the pro-
　　　 cess of

算日子　suàn rìzi (VO) reckon up the
　　　 days; work out what
　　　 day it is

日子　rìzi (N) day, date, special day

万里长城　Wànlǐ Chángchéng (PW) the
　　　 Great Wall

里　lǐ (M) 1 lǐ 里 = ½ km
　　　 (公里 gōnglǐ, 'km';
　　　 英里 yīnglǐ, 'mile')

正　zhèng (A) just then, just at that
　　　 point

毛毛雨　máomáoyǔ (N) drizzle

渐渐(地)　jiànjiàn(de) (A) gradually

黑　hēi (SV) black; dark

-下来　-xialai (V/SV comp) down, to a
　　　 halt, increasingly, etc.

低　dī (SV) low
　　　 (V) droop

屋子　wūzi (N) room

160

来回来去(地) láihuí láiqù(de) (A) backwards and forwards

-起来 -qilai (V/SV comp) begin, come to, etc.

每隔 měigé (CV) at intervals of; every (so often)

隔 gé (V) isolate, separate, cut off

正在 zhèngzài (A) just ——ing

要紧 yàojǐn (SV) important, urgent

自从 zìcóng (CV) ever since

年轻人 niánqīng rén (N) young person

单枪匹马 dānqiāng-pǐmǎ (set phrase) 'single spear one horse': singlehanded

枪 qiāng (N) spear; gun

电报 diànbào (N) telegram

会 huì (MV) would, be sure to; be likely to

报告 bàogào (V/N) report

一切 yíqiè (N) everything; all, every

从...起 cóng ... qǐ starting from ...

紧张 jǐnzhāng (SV) tense, tight, nervous; in short supply

铃 líng (N) small bell

响 xiǎng (V) sound (SV) loud

赶紧 gǎnjǐn (A) hurriedly

长途 chángtú (AT) long-distance

线 xiàn (N) line, wire, thread

接通 jiētōng (V) connect, put through

喂 wéi, wèi (I) hello! hey!

雪 xuě (N) snow

下雪 xià-xuě (V-O) to snow

零下 língxià (PW) below zero

度 dù (M) degree

故宫 Gùgōng (PW) (former palace) the Palace Museum

旅馆 lǚguǎn (N) hotel

伟大 wěidà (SV) great, imposing, mighty

进行 jìnxíng (V) go on, be under way; carry on, carry out

方面 fāngmiàn (N) aspect, respect, side, quarter

联系 liánxì (V) get in contact with (N) contact, link

有关 yǒu-guān (SV) relevant, (the one) concerned

帮忙 bāng-máng (V) help

设立 shèlì (V) set up, establish

办事处 bànshìchù (N) bureau

下去 -xiaqu (V/SV comp) continue, carry on

手续 shǒuxù (N) procedures, formality

旅费 lǚfèi (N) travel expenses

镑 bàng (M) pound (sterling)

毛病 máobìng (N) fault, defect, shortcomings

病 bìng (N) illness

出毛病 chū máobìng (VO) develop a fault

排队 pái-duì (V-O) line up, queue up

电影院 diànyǐngyuàn (PW) cinema

盘子 pánzi (N) plate, tray

161

这是一间相当大的办公室.一进门左边儿放着一套沙发,右边儿立着一排书架.四面墙上挂着好几幅中国山水.离窗户不远有一张办公桌.上头除了两个颜色不同的电话以外,只摆着一个绿色的大烟灰缸.桌子后头坐着一位头发灰白,戴着眼镜儿,穿着西服的中年人.他就是这家华侨贸易公司的钱总经理.这时候他一边儿抽着烟,一边儿看着对面墙上的月历,不知道他是在算日子还是在看月历上的那幅万里长城.窗外正下着毛毛雨.天渐渐地黑下来了.钱总经理抽完烟,站起来把灯开开以后,就低着头在屋子里来回来去地走起来了.可是每隔两三分钟,他的眼睛就要看看桌儿上的电话.对了,他正在等一个非常要紧的电话.自从公司的小万去中国以后,他天天都在着急,不知道这位平常爱玩儿的年轻人单枪匹马能不能把事情办好.昨天接到他的电报说一、两天就会打电话回来,报告一切.所以今天从早晨起钱总经理就一直在紧张地等着......

忽然电话铃响了,他赶紧跑过去接.果然是小万来的长途电话.线接通了以后:

A:喂!总经理吗?我是万通啊!

B:喂!小万吗?我正在等你的电话呢!北京怎么样啊?

A:冷得不得了,现在正在下大雪呢.零下十二度!

B:一切都没问题吧?

A:没问题!冷是冷,风景可是真漂亮.故宫,北海离我住的旅馆都不远,我已经去过好几次了.真是不到北京不知道中国的伟大!

B：我是问你公司的事情有没有问题,你怎么谈起风景来了?

A：噢!公司的事情啊?还在进行呢.各方面都联系得差不多了,有关单位都很帮忙,看起来是不会有什么问题的.

B：那就好!喂,小万,在北京设立办事处的事有希望吗?

A：有是有,不过现在北京房子相当紧张,找起来很不容易,恐怕还得多等些时候.

B：可是一直等下去也不是办法啊!喂,你打算什么时候去上海?

A：我正在办手续呢,这儿的事一完,马上就飞上海.噢,对了,总经理,有一件事得请您帮忙.

B：什么事啊?你说吧!

A：我的旅费差不多快用完了,公司能不能先借给我五百镑?

B：喂,你说什么?我听不清楚啊!

A：我说我的旅费快用完了,想跟公司借五百镑.

B：喂,喂,你说什么?我一句都听不清楚,大概是线出毛病了,小万,下次再谈吧!

SKETCHES

(1) A：喂,景山公司吗?

　　B：找谁啊?

　　A：小黄在吗?

　　B：我就是.你哪位?

　　A：听不出来啊?你猜猜吧!

　　B：欸,我正忙着呢,没工夫跟你猜着玩儿,找我有什么事吗?

　　A：没事就不能找你了?好,跟你说吧,我上午排了半天队才搞到两张票,明天晚上想不想看电影儿?

B：好啊,我明天晚上正好没事儿,在哪儿啊?

A：就在离我们厂不远的那个电影院,七点钟老地方见吧.

B：喂喂,等一等,我还没搞清楚你是谁呢.

A：什么?你真不知道我是谁啊?小黄,你再想想上星期天......

B：小黄?我不是小黄,我姓王,我们这儿连半个姓黄的都没有.

A：你们不是景山公司吗?

B：不是,我们这儿是青山公司,你打错了!

A：打错了?!那....你为什么要接呢?

(2)　　　离现在已经有两千多年了,有一天在中国北方离海边儿不远的一条路上,有人听见两个小孩儿正在谈有关太阳的问题:

A：欸,我忽然想起一个问题来:你说太阳什么时候离我们最近?

B：当然早晨离我们最近.

A：为什么呢?

B：你看早晨太阳刚出来的时候多么大,慢慢儿地越来越小,到了中午只有盘子那么大了.东西离我们越远,看起来就越小,这不是很简单吗?!

A：我看不完全对吧.

B：为什么呢?

A：你看早晨太阳出来的时候,我们一点儿也不觉得热,可是到了中午就热起来了.平常不是离火越近越觉得热吗?所以我说我们中午离太阳最近.

SPEECH PATTERNS

(1) The progressive aspect

(a) Sentence particle ne

1. 他在屋子里干吗呢？　打电话呢.
2. 你弟弟呢？　在楼上睡觉呢.
3. 他们俩做什么呢？　看小说呢.
4. 老李怎么还没来？　他在街上买东西呢.

(b) Zhèng ... (ne)

1. 我们正说他呢,他就来了.
2. 他们正吃饭呢,我们在外头等一会儿吧.
3. 我进门的时候,墙上的钟正打十二点呢.
4. 雨正大呢,吃了饭再走吧.
5. 今天早晨我正走过文化宫门口的时候,听见后头有人叫我.....
6. 我正急得不知道怎么办的时候,电话铃响了.
7. 老李呢？　快去,快去,他正在办公室等你呢!
8. 那些学生正在那儿谈天说地呢!

(c) Zài ... (ne)

1. 最近很多人都在谈年轻人抽烟的问题.
2. 我在跟你说话,你听见了没有？　什么?你说什么?
3. 他这些年一直在研究为什么吃中国菜不容易胖.
4. 风在吹,雨在下,我什么时候才能回家?
5. 我刚才还在说不要红的,你怎么又给了我一个红的?
6. 你在忙什么？　我天天都在作报告,一个完了,又来一个.
7. 他每天都在为三顿饭着急,总是在打算怎么跟人借钱.
8. 他没(有)在学习,他在看电视呢.
9. 她不是在写字,是在画画儿.

165

(d) <u>Zhèngzài</u> ... (<u>ne</u>)

1. 我们进办公室的时候,他正在打电话呢.
2. 去中国教书的事有希望吗?　正在进行呢.
3. 你正在干吗呢?能不能来帮帮忙?
   我正在写一封很要紧的信,写完了就来.
4. 喂,总机,接通了没有?　你别着急,正在给您接呢. (总机,
   'exchange')
5. 这两天他怎么这么用功?　他正在预备考试呢.
6. 他是不是正在办公呢?　没有,他正在跟朋友打牌呢.
7. 他正在忙吗?　没有,正在休息呢.
8. 我进来的时候你正在跟谁说话?　我没跟谁说话,我正在练
   习第十六课的对话呢. (对话, 'dialogue')

(2) The continuous aspect

(a) Main verb with <u>-zhe</u>

1. 老王干吗呢?　他在沙发上坐着呢.
2. 他手上拿着什么呢?　我也看不清楚,好象是一把手枪.
3. 要不要我跟你一块儿进去?　不必了,你就在这儿等着我吧.
4. 你朋友找着房子了吗?　还没呢,还在旅馆住着呢.
5. 别老低着头! 看着我!
6. 别站着,快坐下来,后头的人要说话了.
7. 里头说着话呢,你在外头等几分钟吧.
8. 你别老坐着,每隔半小时应该站起来走走.
9. 他心里一直在想着钱的问题.
10. 你一个人去得带着枪吧!

(b) V-<u>zhe</u> indicating a settled state that results from the original
    action of the verb

1. 沙发上坐着两个人,一胖一瘦,都戴着眼镜儿.
2. 办公桌上放着不少东西,就是没有烟灰缸.
3. 你快出去看看,门外头站着一个中年人,说是要找你.

166

4. 这简直不象一间办公室,窗户上贴着旧报,墙上挂着前年的月历。
5. 桌子中间放着一个大碗,碗上画着一条长龙。
6. 这间屋子里一共住着多少人?
7. 这么冷,快把窗户关上吧! 窗户本来就是关着的,没开着。
8. 你看旅馆门口的地上写着四个大白字:'不准 —— 什么?'

(c) V/SV-zhe used in a subordinate role

1. 你说怎么去? 路不远,走着去吧。
2. 这件事我一个人做不了,你得帮着我做。 好,没问题。
3. 她正在做饭吧? 没有,你看她在那儿坐着看报呢。
4. 你吃完再说吧,吃着东西说话,不太好看。
5. 街上汽车这么多,你不能低着头走路。
6. 妈说不准吃着饭看书,你不知道吗?
   我没有吃着饭看书,我看着书吃饭也不行吗?
7. 你怎么一个人关着门喝酒,朋友都不要了?
8. 忙什么呢? 我正忙着跟各方面联系呢。
9. 他怎么只吃了一口饭就跑了? 他急着要到火车站去接朋友。
10. 她一发现说错了话,马上就红着脸跑出去了。
11. 母亲拉着孩子的手说:"别怕,你一定可以做好的!"
12. 我们几个人一边儿走着,一边儿说着,很快就到了。
13. 抽着烟,喝着酒,大家高兴极了。
14. 他一边儿跑着,一边儿叫着,街上的人都在看他。
15. 她一边儿跟我说着话,一边儿就把菜炒好了。

(3) Distance

Patterns: a.　　A　　lí　　B　　yuǎn/jìn
　　　　　　　他家　离　公司　远不远?
　　　　　b.　　A　　lí　　B　(yǒu)　NU　M　(lù/dì)
　　　　　　　伦敦　离　北京　有　几千公里?
　　　　　c.　　A　　lí　　B　　yǒu NU M N
　　　　　　　现在　离　上班时间还有　三分钟。

1. 办公室离家远吗？　　很近,我就住在办公室的楼上.
2. 故宫离这儿有多远？　　不远,从这儿往东一直走,十分钟就到.
3. 你住的旅馆在哪儿？　　在城外,离这儿最少有八公里.
4. 他家离车站比我家离车站大概远半英里.
5. 她住的地方离北海公园只有几分钟的路.
6. 我们公社离南京大概有三百里地.
7. 那件事离现在有多久了？　　已经有七、八年了吧,没人记得了.
8. 快下课了吧？　下课?现在才十点半,离下课还有二十分钟呢.

(4) Extended use of directional complements

Patterns: a. 我们正在路上的时候,忽然下起雪来了. (start to)
b. 他们工厂的办事处已经办起来了. (in operation)
c. 这个问题研究起来非常有意思. (when you come to)
d. 中文越来越难,我实在学不下去了. (carry on)
e. 这是谁唱的歌儿,你听出来了吗? (detect)
f. 火车快到站了,你看已经慢下来了. (progressive)

1. 奇怪,今天又冷起来了,多少度啊?
2. 快考试了,学生都紧张起来了.
3. 我们一说他正在搞对象,他的脸马上就红起来了.
4. 线还没接通,他就说起话来了.
5. 别人还没吃完饭,他就抽起烟来了.
6. 他真能干,一个人就把办事处搞起来了.
7. 忘了自己的电话多少号?!你再想想!
   啊,我想起来了:四四 七三二六.
8. 他们把那个地方隔起来了,不准人进去. (隔起来, 'set apart, cordon off')
9. 这件事啊,说起来容易,做起来难.
10. 他弟弟看起来很聪明,可是念起书来笨得跟牛一样.
11. 算起来我已经有三年没吃过中国饭了.
12. 比起他们来我差远了.　　你别客气了!

13. 看起来天气还要冷下去。

14. 走吧,别听了!再听下去我就要睡着了。 我已经睡了一觉了。

15. 她一看见老师来了,紧张得说不下去了。

16. 信寄不到,电话打不通谁能想出办法来?

17. 他穿着西服,戴着太阳眼镜儿,我没认出他来。

18. 我花了三天的工夫才把这个报告写出来。

19. 天渐渐黑下来了,路上的车也越来越少了。

20. 他已经把经理的工作接下来了。

(5) The concessive form of 'X shi X'

Pattern: 这张山水画儿不错吧?   不错是不错,就是太贵了。

1. 你单枪匹马一个人去,不怕吗?   怕是怕,可是不去不行。

2. 这种电视机太贵了!   贵是贵一点儿,可是东西实在好。

3. 你还学不学?   学是学,不过想换个地方。

4. 你想到中国去旅行吗?   想是想,可是没人给我出旅费。

5. 你不买了吗?   我买还是要买,不过不买这种颜色的。

6. 你给他打电话了吗?   打是打了,不过没打通。

7. 她去过上海吗?

   去是去过,不过那时候她才三个月,什么都不知道。

8. 你没带着枪吗?   带是带着呢,可是不知道怎么用。

(6) The modal verb 'huì'

1. 你看今天会不会下雨?   大概不会吧。

2. 这件事一定是他干的!

   不会的,他那么聪明的人,不会干这种笨事。

3. 我真不明白,他怎么会连北京的'京'字都不会写!

4. 看起来雪不会很快就停的。

5. 如果你不照着我的话做,就一定会出毛病。

6. 他不高兴,不会是因为我没借钱给他吧。

列	liè (V) to list (M) a row of	让	ràng [讓] (V) to yield; to allow (CV) by (in passive construc- tions)

奔	bēn
	(LC) to run, to rush
	(V) to go to, to be bound
	    for
		凉	liáng [涼]
			(SV) cool, cold
			凉快 pleasantly cool (of
			      weather)

夜	yè * night (M) a night	爽	shuǎng (SV) crisp, refreshing
河	hé (N) river (M:条)	秋	qiū * autumn 秋天
无	wú [無] (LC) not to have; there is not; without (AT) -less	踪	zōng * footprint, trace, tracks
际	jì * [際] border, boundary, edge; interval; between; occasion 国际 international	言	yán * speech; word 语言 language
蓝	lán [藍] (SV) blue a surname	播	bō (V) to sow (seeds); to spread; to broadcast
空	kōng * sky 天空; air 空气 (SV) empty, hollow, void	醒	xǐng (V) to awake; to regain con- sciousness; to sober up
被	bèi (CV) by (in passive construc- tions) (N) quilt	阔	kuò [闊] * wide (SV) rich, ostentatious

洗	xǐ
	(V) to wash; to develop (
	    photographs); to shuffle
	    (cards)
		吸	xī
			(V) to inhale; to absorb
			吸烟 = 抽烟

净	jìng [淨] * clean 干净 (A) merely; nothing but	引	yǐn (V) to draw; to lead; to attract
闷	mēn [悶] (SV) stuffy, close	相	xiàng (N) looks, appearance; phys- iognomy 照相 to take photographs

寻	xún * [尋] to look for, to search for	拦	lán [攔] (V) to bar, to block, to hold back
物	wù * (LC) thing (an object or article); substance	代	dài (V) to substitute for; to take the place of (CV) for
骡	luó * [騾] mule 骡子 (M:匹) 骡马 mules and horses	表	biǎo * surface; to show, to express; -meter (N) a table, list, form
劳	láo * [勞] toil, labour; tired; to trouble a surname	兴	xing [興] * to prosper, to rise, to start (V) to become popular
动	dòng [動] (V) to move; to use; to start 劳动 to work, labour(ing)	奋	fèn * [奮] to exert oneself, to put forth effort
留	liú (V) to retain, to keep, to remain 留学 study abroad	汗	hàn (N) sweat, perspiration 出汗 (V-O) to sweat
提	tí (V) to lift (from above), to carry; to mention; to propose	港	gǎng (N) harbour, port 香港 Hong Kong
土	tǔ (N) earth, soil, dust (AT) local (SV) uncouth	护	hù [護] (V) to protect 护照 passport
验	yàn [驗] (V) to examine, to test 经验 (N/V) experience	偷	tōu (V) to steal 小偷(儿) petty thief
亿	yì [億] (NU) hundred million 亿万 hundreds of millions	厕	cè * [廁] lavatory 厕所 男厕(所) Gents 女厕(所) Ladies
终	zhōng * [終] end, finish	误	wù * [誤] error, erroneous; to miss (a train, etc.); by mistake
于	yú * [於] (LC) at, in; in regard to 终于 at (long) last	托	tuō [託] (V) to entrust; to ask sb. to do sth. for one
台	tái [臺] (N) terrace, raised platform, stage short for Taiwan 台湾	箱	xiāng * chest, box, case (M) chest/box/trunk of

冬	dōng　　　* winter 冬天	颐	yí　　　*　[頤] cheek; to nourish 颐和园　the Summer Palace (outside Peking)
卫	wèi　　　*　[衛] to defend, to guard, to pro- tect 卫生 hygiene　　a surname	座	zuò * seat 座位 ; pedestal (M) for mountains, bridges, 　　buildings, etc.
纸	zhǐ　　　　　[紙] (N) paper　　　　(M:张)	桥	qiáo　　　　[橋] (N) bridge　　　(M:座)
打	dá (M) dozen (transliteration)	孔	kǒng (N) hole, aperture a surname　　孔子 Confucius

STROKE—ORDER

列　一 厂 歹 歹 列 列　　　　播　扌 扩 扩 扩 护 捽 捽 採 播

奔　大 本 本 李 奔　　　　　　醒　一 西 西 酉 酲 醒

夜　一 广 疒 疗 夜 夜　　　　阔　门 门 阔 阔

河　氵 氵 汀 河 河　　　　　　吸　口 口 叹 吸

无　一 二 于 无　　　　　　　　引　丨 弓 弓 引

际　阝 阝 阡 际　　　　　　　　相　木 杓 相 相

蓝　一 艹 艹 蓝 萨 莎 莓 蓝 蓝　寻　コ ヨ ヨ 寻

空　宀 宀 空 空　　　　　　　　物　丿 牛 牛 牝 物

被　丶 衤 衤 衤 礻 衤 衤 衤 被 被　骡　丁 马 马 驲 骡

洗　氵 氵 汼 汼 浐 洴 洗　　　　劳　艹 艹 芧 劳

净　冫 冫 汐 沪 净 净 净　　　　动　二 云 云 动 动

闷　丶 冫 门 闷 闷　　　　　　　留　丿 乚 丩 幻 邸 留

让　讠 让 让 让　　　　　　　　提　扌 押 捍 捍 捍 提

凉　冫 广 沽 凉　　　　　　　　土　一 十 土

爽　一 厂 乊 歹 歪 歪 爽 爽 爽　验　马 马 驳 驳 验 验

秋　二 千 禾 禾 秒 秋　　　　　亿　亻 亿

踪　口 口 甲 甲 足 跅 跠 踪　　终　纟 纟 纱 纹 终

言　二 言 言　　　　　　　　　　于　一 二 于

172

台　ㄥ　厶　台
拦　扌　扌　拦
代　亻　亻　代　代
表　二　卅　主　丰　丰　表　表
兴　丶　丷　丷　兴　兴
奋　一　大　奋　奋
汗　氵　汗　汗
港　氵　氵　沣　洪　洪　港　港　港
护　扌　扌　护　护　护
偷　亻　亻　价　价　偷　偷
厕　一　厂　厂　厕　厕

误　讠　讠　误　误
记　讠　讠　记
箱　竹　竹　箱
冬　丶　勹　夂　冬
卫　フ　卫　卫
纸　纟　纟　纟　纸　纸
打　扌　打
颐　丆　匝　臣　臣　臣　颐　颐
座　亠　广　庐　庐　座　座
桥　木　杦　杦　桥　桥
孔　フ　了　子　孔

VOCABULARY

天亮　tiānliàng (S-Predicate) day-break (lit: sky bright)

列车　lièchē (N) train (rail-way term)

奔　bēn (V) rush, speed

(黑)夜　(hēi)yè (N) (dark) night

黄河　Huánghé (PR) Yellow River

车窗　chēchuāng (N) carriage win-dow

望　wàng (V) look into the distance, look across at

南方　nánfāng (PW) the south

青山绿水　qīngshān lǜshuǐ (set phrase) verdant hills and green waters

眼前　yǎnqián (PW) before the eyes

一望无际　yí wàng wújì (set phrase) 'look afar no bound' — as far as the eye can see

华北平原　Huáběi Píngyuán (PW) North China Plain

蓝色　lán(sè) (SV) blue (coloured)

天空　tiānkōng (N) sky

被　bèi (CV) by (in passive con-structions)

洗　xǐ (V) wash

明净　míngjìng (SV) bright and clean, luminous

闷热　mēnrè (SV/N) sultry; sultriness

让　ràng (V) let, allow
　　(CV) by (in passive con-structions)

凉爽　liángshuǎng (SV) cool and refreshing

秋风　qiūfēng (N) autumn wind (= 秋天的风)

无影无踪　wúyǐng wúzōng (set phrase) without shadow with-out trace

北京语言学院　Běijīng Yǔyán Xué-yuàn (PR) Peking Languages Institute

同车　tóngchē (N) 'same car': fellow (of travellers)

旅客　lǚkè (N) traveller, passenger

清早　qīngzǎo (TW) early morning

广播 guǎngbō (N/V) broadcast

醒 xǐng (V) awake(n)

  叫醒 jiàoxǐng (V) 'call awake' wake up

立刻 lìkè (A) immediately

开阔 kāikuò (SV) wide, open (of spaces)

景色 jǐngsè (N) landscape, scenery, scene

吸引 xīyǐn (V) attract, draw

照相 zhào xiàng (VO) take photograph

  照相机 zhàoxiàngjī (N) camera

更是 gèngshi (A) further, on top of that

不停地 bùtíngde (A) unceasingly

寻找 xúnzhǎo (V) seek, look for

镜头 jìngtóu (N) shot (photography); camera lens

地里 dì-lǐ (PW) in the fields

农作物 nóngzuòwù (N) farm crops

骡马大车 luó-mǎ dàchē (adjunct + N) mule and horse carts

劳动 láodòng (V/N) labour (physical)

社员 shèyuán (N) member of a shè (society, association, commune)

照下来 zhàoxialai (V) get on film

所 suǒ (A) 'which'

对(他们)来说 duì (tāmen) lai shuō (PH) 'come to speak regarding (them)' — as far as (they) are concerned

新奇 xīnqí (SV) novel

亲切 qīnqiè (SV) close and dear, familiar

留学 liúxué (V) study abroad

  留 liú (V) remain

提高 tígāo (V) raise, heighten, improve

了解 liǎojiě (V) understand

下 xià (M) a 'go' (verbal measure)

风土人情 fēngtǔ rénqíng (set phrase) local conditions (human and environmental)

实际 shíjì (SV/A) real(ly), actual(ly), concrete(ly)

体验 tǐyàn (V) experience for oneself

亿 yì (NU) hundred million

日常 rìcháng (SV) everyday, routine

难忘 nán-wàng (SV) memorable

上课 shàng kè (VO) give a lesson

铁路 tiělù (N) railway

房屋 fángwū (collective N) houses, buildings

终于 zhōngyú (A) finally, at last

站台 zhàntái (N) railway platform

拦住 lánzhù (V) stop, bar the way

代表 dàibiǎo (V) represent (CV) on behalf of (N) representative

不敢当 bù gǎn dāng (IE) unworthy of the honour; be flattered; would not presume

接 jiē (V) meet (on arrival)

兴奋 xīngfèn (SV) excited

凉快 liángkuai (SV) pleasantly cool

汗 hàn (N) sweat

  一身汗 yì shēn hàn (NU M N) sweating all over

秋高气爽 qiū-gāo qì-shuǎng (set phrase) autumn (sky) high and air bracing — clear and refreshing autumn weather

信 xìn (V) believe

香港 Xiānggǎng (PW) Hong Kong

护照 hùzhào (N) passport

钱包 qiánbāo (N) purse, wallet

叫 jiào (CV) by (in passive constructions)

偷 tōu (V) steal

-走 -zou (V comp) away

厕所 cèsuǒ (N) lavatory

上厕所 shàng cèsuǒ (VO) go to lavatory

结果 jiéguǒ (N) result, outcome (MA) as a result, consequently

误 wù (V) miss (train, bus, etc.)

班 bān (M) for scheduled journeys by public transport

真是! zhēnshi!(I) well really! the idea! bad show!

行李 xíngli (N) luggage

托运 tuōyùn (V) book/check through (baggage)

全 quán (A) entirely, completely (=完全) (SV) complete, whole, entire

手提包 shǒutíbāo (N) (hand)bag, hold-all

箱子 xiāngzi (N) suitcase, trunk, box

冬天 dōngtiān (TW) winter

衣服 yīfu (N) clothing, clothes

到时候 dào shíhou (PH) when the time comes

打字机 dǎzìjī (N) typewriter

口香糖 kǒuxiāngtáng (N) chewing gum

卫生纸 wèishēngzhǐ (N) toilet paper

卫生 wèishēng (N) hygiene (SV) hygienic

纸 zhǐ (N) paper

得了 déle (IE) that's enough, pack it in

说 shuō (V) reprove, criticize

打 dá (M) dozen

顿 dùn (M) measure for beating

动 dòng (V) move, touch

双数 shuāngshù (N) even number

单数 dānshù (N) odd number

照片 zhàopiàn (N) photograph

颐和园 Yíhéyuán (PW) Summer Palace (outside Peking)

座 zuò (M) for bridges, mountains, etc.

桥 qiáo (N) bridge

十七孔桥 Shíqī kǒng Qiáo (PR) Seventeen Arch (lit: aperture) Bridge

借用 jièyòng (V) borrow for use, turn to some purpose, take up

一课书 yí kè shū (NU M N) a written lesson

隔开 gékāi (V) separate

连 lián (V) join, connect

PRESENTATION

天亮了！列车奔过了黑夜,也奔过了黄河！从车窗望出去,南方的青山绿水已经看不见了,眼前是一望无际的华北平原.蓝色的天空象被水洗过一样的明净,昨晚的闷热也让凉爽的秋风吹得无影无踪.那几个要到北京语言学院去学习的英国学生昨天一天忙着跟同车的旅客谈天儿,夜里又没睡好.清早被车上的广播叫醒以后,本来还想再睡一会儿,但是一看窗外,立刻就让这开阔的景色吸引住了.爱照相的更是拿出照相机,不停地寻找镜头;地里的农作物,路上的骡马大车,正在劳动的公社社员都被他们照下来了.这几个年轻人已经在伦敦大学念过了一年中文,现在所看到的对他们来说是那么新奇,又是那么亲切.他们来留学,一方面是要提高自己的汉语水平,一方面也是想了解一下中国各地的风土人情,实际体验一下十亿人的日常生活.火车上这三十多小时已经给他们上了难忘的一课.

列车渐渐地慢下来了,铁路两旁的房屋越来越多,终于北京站到了.这几个英国同学刚下车,站台那边儿就走过来一位戴眼镜儿的中年人把他们拦住了：

DIALOGUE

王：你们几位是英国来的同学吧?我姓王,代表北京语言学院来欢迎你们！

李：真不敢当！王老师,您好！谢谢您来接我们.

王：不客气！你们大家好！怎么样,坐了两夜一天的火车,够累了吧?

李：我们也许是太兴奋了,一点儿也不觉得累.北京天气真好,比南方凉快多了.前天在广州从早到晚都是一身汗,脑子都给热糊涂了.

王：北京已经热过了，现在正是秋高气爽的好时候。欸，你们一共不是九个人吗？还有两位呢？

李：说出来您也许不信，我们那两个同学，一个在香港坐公共汽车，护照、钱包都叫人给偷走了，现在还在找呢；另外一个在广州车站，开车以前跑去上厕所，结果误了这班车。

王：欸！真是！希望他们明后天能到。等会儿我再跟广州联系一下儿。你们行李都拿下来了吗？有托运的没有？

李：我们六个人的行李全都在这儿。白海伦除了这三个大手提包以外，还有几件托运的。

王：你们六个人都是一个小箱子啊？冬天的衣服带了吗？

李：我们想实际体验一下儿中国的生活，决定衣食住行都要跟中国同学一样，没有的东西到时候再买，所以行李很少。

王：那太好了！白同学有几件托运的行李啊？

白：我……

李：她大概不好意思说，一共六大件，您没想到吧！从自行车到打字机；从口香糖到卫生纸，要什么有什么！

白：得了，得了，小李，我带什么用不着你替我广播，你先让王老师看看你的箱子再说别人吧！

李：我就这么一个小箱子，有什么好看的？

白：外头是没什么好看，可是里头呢？整整两打咖啡！你要体验中国生活带咖啡来干吗？

李：我……我每天早晨不喝咖啡醒不了，要是醒不了怎么能去体验生活呢？！

(1) A: 雪华,雪华,你来一下儿好吗?

　　B: 什么事啊?我正在炒菜呢!这回又是什么东西找不着了?

　　A: 你看见我那张地图没有?本来放在桌子上,不知道叫谁给拿走了?

　　B: 昨天晚上你跟老黄看着地图谈旅行,是不是让他借去了?

　　A: 没有,没有,老黄地图多得很,我那张就是他送的。

　　B: 会不会叫小明拿去玩儿了?你问问他。

　　A: 这孩子上次玩儿我的小计算机,不是叫我好好儿地打了一顿吗?
　　　我想他不敢再动我的东西了吧.你再帮我想想。

　　B: 你看风这么大,窗户又没关,也许让风给吹跑了。

　　A: 桌子上那么多纸都没吹走,地图更吹不走了。

　　B: 你早上没带到学校去吗?

　　A: 噢!学校?对了!我想起来了,我已经把地图挂在办公室的墙
　　　上了.真是这天气!我都给热糊涂了!

　　B: 你的脑子哪天清楚啊?!

(2) A: 时间过得真快,没想到我们已经学了半年的中文了。

　　B: 是啊!这本书马上就要学完了。

　　A: 你觉得这本书怎么样?

　　B: 我觉得相当不错,不过有一点我不明白:为什么不多不少十七课?

　　A: 十七课不行吗?

　　B: 行当然行,不过平常不是十六、十八就是二十、二十四,都是双数,
　　　很少有单数的。

　　A: 本来我也奇怪这件事,后来看到一张颐和园的照片才明白。

　　B: 颐和园?这本书跟颐和园有什么关系?

　　A: 你忘了:颐和园不是有一座很漂亮的桥吗?

　　B: 你是说那座闻名世界的十七孔桥?

　　A: 对了!就是十七孔桥!写这本书的人大概是借用这个意思,希
　　　望这十七课书能象一座桥一样,把被语言隔开的外国人民
　　　和中国人民连在一起!

SPEECH PATTERNS

(1) <u>Passive constructions</u>

(a) Passive in English, not in Chinese

1. 电报收到了,信还没收到呢.
2. 我的护照已经拿到了,别的手续正在办呢.
3. 在中国留学一年,他的汉语水平大大地提高了.
4. 汽车洗过了以后,看起来跟新的一样.
5. 今天的糖醋鱼真不错,你看,连鱼头都吃了.
6. 行李送来了吗？　　箱子已经送来了,手提包还没呢.
7. 这条新闻已经广播到全世界了.
8. 秋天的晚上她常常站在海边儿,吹着海风,想着以前的事.
9. 老王的自行车已经找到了.（是谁找到的？　不知道.)
   cf.老王已经找到他的自行车了.
10. 东西都搬走了吗？
    cf.他们都搬走了吗？

(b) With coverbs of agent '<u>bèi</u>', '<u>jiào</u>', '<u>ràng</u>' and '<u>gěi</u>'

Patterns: a.　　receiver　<u>bèi</u>　V

　　　　　　小王　　被　打了.

　　　　　b.　　receiver　CVs of agent　doer (<u>gěi</u>)　V

　　　　　　小王　　被/叫/让　　人（给）打了.

　　　　　c.　　receiver　<u>gěi</u>　doer　V

　　　　　　小王　　给　人　打了.

1. 他们都被请去了.
2. 我们都被留在那儿了.
3. 他已经被拉上来了.
4. 他被问得说不出话来了.
5. 我们被关在一间黑屋子里,连厕所都不准上.
6. 你的照相机能不能借我用一天？　　对不起,已经被人借走了.
7. 我昨天买的口香糖呢？　　都叫孩子给吃了.
8. 你的行李呢？　　找不着了,大概被人拿错了.

179

9. 我一下车就被两个外国人拦住了。
10. 他们一家人坐在那儿,全叫电视给吸引住了。
11. 我正要用的那张纸让风给吹到树上去了。
12. 这件事如果让他知道了,一定会替你广播出去。
13. 他的护照飞机票都叫人偷走了吗?　没有,只有钱被偷了。
14. 快进去吧,外头这么冷,别让风给吹病了。
15. 你这么糊涂,恐怕给人卖了都不知道。

(2) <u>Three types of sentences compared</u>

   (a) Simply tells what happened
   (b) Says what someone/something did with someone/something
   (c) Says what happened to someone/something

1a. 他喝了一杯茶就走了。
 b. 他把那杯茶喝了。
 c. 那杯茶叫他给喝了。

2a. 他一个人吃了一桌菜,真能吃!
 b. 他一个人把一桌菜都吃了。
 c. 一桌菜都让他一个人给吃了。

3a. 他打了小明一顿。
 b. 小明不听他的话,他把小明打了一顿。
 c. 小明被他打了一顿,心里很不高兴。

4a. 有人偷了他的照相机。
 b. 有人把他的照相机偷走了。
 c. 他的照相机叫人偷走了。

5a. 风吹得我很不舒服。
 b. 风把我吹得很不舒服。
 c. 我被风吹得很不舒服。

6a. 他爱人卖了他的自行车,买了一架照相机。
 b. 因为没钱买菜,他爱人把他的自行车卖了。
 c. 他的自行车呢?　他的自行车叫他爱人给卖了。

(3) Appearance and disappearance

1. 你看,那边儿飞过来一个什么东西?
2. 我们那条路上搬走了一家美国人,搬来了两家德国人.
3. 太白山上发现了很多两千年以前的东西.
4. 我们公司最近走了不少人.
5. 昨天我听说图书馆里新到了五千本中文书.
6. 奇怪,我钱包里怎么少了五块钱?
7. 我们正在说话,忽然楼上走下来一位穿蓝衣服的女学生.
8. 快看!男厕所里走出来一个女孩子.
   那不是女孩子,你别以为头发长的都是女的.

(4) Verbal measures

1. 你在中国坐过几次火车?
2. 这儿的事已经跟他说了三回了,好象他还是不太了解.
3. 他累得不得了,很想去睡一觉.
4. 他只爱舒服不爱劳动,又让他爸爸说了一顿.
5. 我问她找谁,她看了我一眼就走了.
6. 不知道为什么他忽然跑过来打了我三下儿.
7. 我想跟你了解一下儿这儿的风土人情.
8. 我们都应该体验一下儿劳动人民的生活.
9. 他拿起琴来弹了几下儿,好听极了.
10. 我找不着我弟弟了,能不能麻烦您广播一下儿,他名字叫....
11. 明天我不能去欢迎他们,请你代表一下儿行不行?
12. 衣食住行的问题都得好好儿地研究一下儿.

(5) 'YI' for 'whole'

1. 这一手提包的书都是他新买的.
2. 天气这么热,一劳动就是一身汗.
3. 电话响了,快去替我接一下儿,我正在洗碗,一手的水.

4. 你看他一身的雪,真象个大雪人儿.
5. 一飞机的旅客都叫窗外的景色吸引住了.
6. 谁在这儿洗东西了?怎么搞得一地都是水?
7. 一屋子的酒都叫他儿子给喝了.
8. 一车的照相机都叫人给偷了.

(6) 'Zai' for action deferred

1. 今天太晚了,明天再去办吧!
   (cf. 今天没办好,明天还要再去办.)
2. 这件事应该怎么办? 等他来了再说吧!
3. 我想买点儿卫生纸. 家里有那么多,用完了再买吧.
4. 我得去问问他. 他还在睡觉呢,等他醒了再问他吧.
5. 经不经过香港,你们研究一下儿再决定吧.
6. 我跟他们联系以后再打电话给你,好不好?
7. 你先代表我去车站接他,明天早晨我再到旅馆去看他.
8. 你先把打字学会了,再去找工作就容易多了.

(7) 'Suǒ'

1. 你所看到的都是劳动人民的实际生活.
2. 我们所研究的问题跟电子计算机没什么关系.
3. 我们所能办到的只有这一点.
4. 他们所用的法子听说是最特别的.
5. 我们大家所希望的就是能把中文学好.

(8) The measure modified

1a. 他一共带了六大件行李,吃的,穿的,什么都有.
 b. 他一共带了六件大行李和两个小手提包.

2a. 这么一小本书就要十镑钱,我不买.
 b. 这本小书对我很有用.

3a. 他送给我们三大包米,够我们吃一年.
 b. 车上有不少肉,还有三包大米. (大米 = 白米)

4a. 做这个菜得用三大碗油.
 b. 做这个菜得用三碗大油. (大油，'lard')

5a. 一进门,左边儿立着一长排书架.
 b. 左边儿是一排很长的书架.

ABBREVIATIONS FOR GRAMMATICAL TERMS

		First appeared in lesson
A	adverb	1
AT	attributive	9
BF	bound form	1
C	conjunction	5
CLV	classificatory verb	2
CV	coverb	9
I	interjection	2
IE	idiomatic expression	1
K	marker	5
L	localizer	8
LC	literary Chinese	3
M	measure	4
MA	movable adverb	4
MV	modal verb	3
N	noun	1
NU	number	3
O	object	3
P	particle	1
PH	phrase	9
PN	pronoun	1
PR	proper noun	9
PW	place word	2
QW	question word	2
S	subject	1
SP	specifier	2
SV	stative verb	1
TW	time word	1
V	verb	3
V-O	verb-object construction	3

VOCABULARY

Figures with entries refer to lesson numbers

a 啊 1	bàn shì 办事 9	bì 币 6
ài 爱 2,3	bànshìchù 办事处 16	bì 必 10
àiren 爱人 2	bāng 帮 16	bìděi 必得 10
ān 安 9	bāng-máng 帮忙 16	bì 毕 11
	bàng 镑 16	bì-yè 毕业 11
	bāo 包 5	biān(r) 边(儿) 8
	bǎo 饱 7	biàn 便 10
bā 八 4	bào 报 5	biǎo 表(錶) 12
bǎ 把 15	bàogào 报告 16	biǎo 表 17
bà 爸 11	bēi 杯 4	bié 别 (SP) 7
bàba 爸爸 11	bēizi 杯子 13	(A) 9
ba 吧 2	běi 北 2,8	biéde (SP) 别的 7
bái 白 13	běibian(r) 北边(儿) 8	biéren 别人 12
báicài 白菜 15	běifāng rén 北方人 12	bìng 病 16
báicài niúròu tāng	Běihǎi Gōngyuán	bìngle 病了 16
白菜牛肉汤 15	北海公园 12	bō 播 17
báiqiējī 白切鸡 15	Běijīng 北京 2	bù/bú 不 1
bǎi 百 9	Běijīng Yǔyán Xuéyuàn	búbì 不必 10
bǎihuò shāngdiàn	北京语言学院 17	bú-cuò 不错 9
百货商店 9	bèi 备 14	bú dàng yì huí shì
bǎi 摆 16	bèi 被 17	不当一回事 15
bān 班(N) 12	bēn 奔 17	búguò 不过 12
(M) 17	běn 本 (M),(SP) 4,14	bú (yào) kèqi
bān 搬 14	běnlái 本来 7	不(要)客气 14
bāndào 搬到 14	bèn 笨 13	búlùn 不论 15
bàn 半 5	bǐ 笔(N) 5	bùdéliǎo 不得了 13
bàn 办 9	(M) 14	bùgǎndāng 不敢当 17
bànfǎ 办法 12	bǐ 比 13	bù-hǎoyìsi
bàn-gōng 办公 16	bǐfang 比方 13	不好意思 14
bàngōngshì 办公室 16	bǐfang shuō 比方说 13	bù shūfu 不舒服 10
bàngōngzhuō 办公桌 16	bǐjiào 比较 13	bùtíng(de) 不停(地) 17